SEX PROBLEMS

Hari Datt Sharma

V&S PUBLISHERS

Published by:

V&S PUBLISHERS

F-2/16, Ansari Road, Daryaganj, New Delhi-110002
☎ 011-23240026, 011-23240027 • *Fax* 011-23240028
Email info@vspublishers.com • *Website* www.vspublishers.com

Regional Office Hyderabad
5-1-707/1, Brij Bhawan (Beside Central Bank of India Lane)
Bank Street, Koti, Hyderabad - 500 095
☎ 040-24737290
E-mail vspublishershyd@gmail.com

Branch Office Mumbai
Jaywant Industrial Estate, 2nd Floor–222, Tardeo Road
Opposite Sobo Central Mall, Mumbai – 400 034
☎ 022-23510736
E-mail: vspublishersmum@gmail.com

Follow us on:

All books available at **www.vspublishers.com**

© Copyright: **V&S PUBLISHERS**
Edition 2017

The Copyright of this book, as well as all matter contained herein (including illustrations) rests with the Publishers. No person shall copy the name of the book, its title design, matter and illustrations in any form and in any language, totally or partially or in any distorted form. Anybody doing so shall face legal action and will be responsible for damages.

Printed at : Repro Knowledgecast Limited, Thane

Contents

	Preface	5
1.	Male Sex Organs	8
2.	Semen is the Seed of the Man	16
3.	Semen Related Problems	24
4.	Female Sex Organs	30
5.	Puberty	37
6.	Menstruation and Menopause	40
7.	Pregnancy	47
8.	Sexual Diseases	58
9.	Birth Control Techniques	67
10.	Sexual Potency	74
11.	Impotence	77
12.	Infertility	81
13.	Aphrodisiacs and Anaphrodisiacs	84
14.	Old-Age Sexual Problems	93
15.	Psychosexual Disorders	96
16.	Common Questions for Adolescents	106

Preface

Many kinds of sexual myths are prevailing throughout the world in many cultures and societies. These are based on misconceptions and fallacies arising out of hearsay, superstitions, bigotry or faulty sexual education. These are the main causes of many psychological sexual problems.

The fact that sex is of fundamental importance, can hardly be overemphasised. Sex is the very foundation of existence. But we can't your the problems misconceptions which comes with sex as they need our utmost attention.

Sex makes some people feel uncomfortable and embarrassed partly because it has been associated for so long with unacceptable and dirty feelings. Sniggering is sometimes a way of covering up these feelings. Embarrassment also comes from the secrecy surrounding the sexual act. Secrets mean you have done something wrong. In societies where sex has been open and free from ideas of guilt; it is accepted much more easily as being normal and natural.

A person may be a millionaire, a world leader, an athlete, a wrestler or a distinguished scientist—but still feels inadequate doing a simple act of sex that is common for animals and birds. It is because animals and birds never think about it. They just respond to changing levels of sex hormones which stimulate or curb their reproductive urge. But in the case of men and women, instincts have been crippled by anxiety resulting from negative preconditioning normally based on expectations of family and norms of the society.

The logic of the various religious leaders is that because sex is necessary to keep the human race going, therefore the sole purpose of sex is reproduction. But it is not accepted by all. You might as well say that since food is necessary to keep the body going, the sole purpose of eating is to stay alive, which won't convince anyone who enjoys rich foods.

If the only purpose of sex were reproduction, nature would have arranged for human females to come on heat only once a year which is sufficient to reproduce the species. While a great deal of sexual activities directly or indirectly relate to reproduction, but having children is not the only purpose of sexual activities. Sex provides release from tension. Sex is stimulating. Any satisfactory sexual experience heightens perception, alleviates boredom and awakens new interests.

Sex offers companionship and intimacy as most of us are afraid of loneliness. Sex can also be used as a weapon. Desired behaviour can be coerced by withholding sex as a punishment or offering it as a reward. Sex is also a form of recreation, available to all classes and conditions of people throughout the world. Pornography, blue movies and dirty jokes are significant form of entertainment. Sex can also be used as an inducement to buy or sell. With such a powerful medium at our disposal, we surely owe it to ourselves to know as much about it as possible.

How you enjoy sex is also a matter of personal preference and is no one else's business. Just as no two people have exactly the same taste in food or clothes, so no two people like exactly the same thing in bed. Perversion is the name we give to other people's variations; to our own we call preference.

For good sex, we need a relaxed and comfortable setting, plenty of good feelings, self-esteem, placing a higher value on own worth. It is a quality which is particularly likely to develop with age and is absolutely necessary for good sexual relationship. But with an increase in number of sexually transmitted diseases, it is necessary for the readers to differentiate between the rights and the wrongs.

Gone are the days when men had to put up with log-like stiff partners. It is now accepted that educated girls have sexual appetites every bit as large as those of men, and have every right to have them satisfied. So, it is not surprising that men feel the pressure on them to perform.

I am sure this book will entirely change your attitude towards sex, and will prove to be an informative, educative and enjoyable reading material for you.

Hari Datt Sharma

Male Sex Organs

Research findings show that some men suffer from an emotional concern that they possess a penis that is abnormally small, a concern based in part on the individual's visual perceptive when looking downwards a flaccid penis, a viewpoint that distorts the true size. The complex may also be supported by the emphasis in literature and other art forms as well as folklore and pornographic material on male genitals that are unusually large.

Myths about the Size of the Penis

Penises vary greatly in shape and it is a myth that a bigger penis is necessarily better. One of the cherished illusions men have about their sexual performance is that the bigger their penis, the better they will satisfy their partner. It is an illusion nourished by pulp fictions and girlie magazines.

The kind of men they read about in novels and stories have penis as hard as iron and as long as a barber's pole, always ready for action. As soon as the penis loses an erection, there is another one raring to go. In these stories, rarely do people come across floppy or remarkably small penises, the kind that droop a little and need coaxing to come into action. Stories of sex with animals by women also confirm their belief in this myth.

The Reality about the Size of the Penis
Despite all the fears and boasts, penis size does not vary markedly from one person to another. There are some large penises around, just as there are some men whose erection can last a long time and return after a short time. But there is far less difference than is generally supposed.

Circumcision
It is a minor operation to remove the foreskin from the man's or boy's penis. This is done for religious reason among Muslim community or sometimes for medical reasons.

Does it make one a better lover if one has been circumcised?

People often think that men who have been circumcised cannot control ejaculation.

Another view is that a circumcised person can continue for longer duration of sexual act than a non-circumcised person. But both these views are myths. During erection, the foreskin usually draws back from the sensitive glans (the head of the penis). So at this stage it is hard to tell if someone has been circumcised.

Being circumcised or not, it makes no difference to the sexual enjoyment.

Small Penis Complex
Sex researchers have found that penises vary in length between 5 to 10 cm when limp, but when they are erect they all average at about 15 cm. Those, that are smaller when relaxed, increase in size more than larger ones. In other words with erection, the difference tends to level out. One erect penis is much the same size as every one else's.

.The Size of the Penis Makes no Difference to Sexual Enjoyment

Forget everything you have been told about penis size. Even if it is undersized, even then it can satisfy the woman better than a big penis. Some men are so obsessed with the idea "bigger is better" that they do not feel adequate even though they are normal. It is now firmly established beyond doubt that penis size makes no difference to women's sexual enjoyment.

Chromosomal Anomalies

About one male in a thousand has a penis which is unusually small due to a chromosomal anomaly. It may have XX rather than XY chromosome sets. In medical language it is known as **Klinefelter's Syndrome**. The extra chromosome means that such individual usually develops feminine breasts and has a low sperm count. They also tend to be obese and display a low level of sexual interest.

There is no relation between **penis size** and **body size**. However there are slight racial differences. Orientals on average have smaller penises than Caucasians. Negroes have larger penises.

However plastic surgeons who perform penis enlargement, report a flourishing business. The results report extension of about one to two inches. It entails releasing the penile shaft from the ligaments and drawing a flap of skin from the pubic area to cover the added length. But it is not worth the time, trouble, money and pain suffered in this connection.

Quacks often Dupe the People

As most people worry about the size of their penis, so charlatans exploit this situation very well to their own advantage. They easily and gladly separate fools from their money for medically approved apparatus or techniques that promise to enlarge penis. Indian quacks prescribe strange types of medicines like massage of the penis with the special oil prepared from a type of lizard *(Sandey-Ka-Tel)*. It is just to befool the people. It does more harm than good.

All the techniques and apparatuses prove ineffective and at worst they can be harmful. Some vacuum like devices can rupture blood vessels in the penis. Sex findings indicate that no pill, potion, exercise, masturbatory technique or external device can affect penis size.

My advice is—Don't worry, feel happy. Your penis is quite normal. When any man who feels anxiety about his penis and reluctantly or hesitantly engages himself in sexual play, the result is the lack of satisfaction.

In evaluating himself, a man must take into consideration his genital inheritance and what physical characteristics his parents and grand-parents handed down to him.

Anatomy of Male Sex Organ

The sex apparatus in a man is only an exterior limb. It is more visible than woman's. The penis is generally less cloaked in mystery. This can be both an advantage as

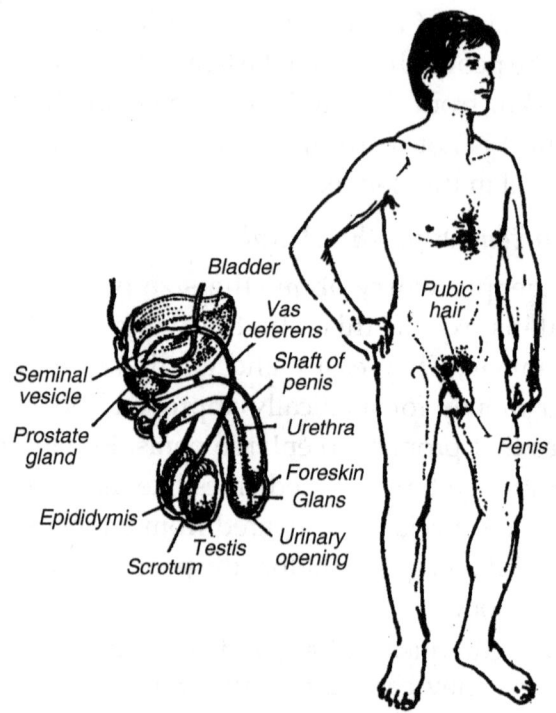

Male reproductive system

well as disadvantage. Penises have an annoying habit of becoming erect at the wrong time and refusing to do so at the right time. They also cause a great deal of anxiety to their owners because of their shape or size.

The biological sexual function of the penis is to penetrate the female vagina and deposit sperm. It is also the urinary outlet. Generally it remains flacid but in response to erotic stimuli it becomes erect and engorged with blood. Erection increases its length and girth. The erection and softening of a penis are fascinating to watch. Both can be brought on by various physical and mental stimuli, but neither is routinely under voluntary control.

Normally it hangs limply downward, but in its erect state it points horizontally outward or slightly upwards at an angle. A penis has no muscles along its length, nor any bone, just a ring of muscles around the base which tightens during sexual excitement and helps to keep it erect.

The Penis

The penis is made up of a long shaft and sensitive tip which is called **glans**. The glans has an opening in it. This is the opening of the **urethra**, a narrow tube which performs the dual function of carrying urine from the bladder and semen from the **vas deferens**—the tube which leads from the **testes**. But it never performs both the functions at the same time. During erection, a small muscle closes off the entrance to the bladder so that no urine can be passed. So it is not possible to pass urine and ejaculate at the same time.

The shaft is covered with loose, wrinkly darkish skin which extends over tip to form the foreskin. The head is studded with a mass of nerve ending which make it the most sensitive part of the penis. The whole of the rim or ridge where the head joins the shaft is capable of providing some very pleasant sensations.

On the underside of the shaft is an exquisitely sensitive area the **ferrum**, which looks like a tightly stretched bowstring. Even the lightest touch applied to this part of the penis is enough to produce an erection.

Scrotum and Testes

The loose pouch of wrinkled skin which hangs down behind the penis and which contains the testes is called the Scrotal sack or Scrotum. It has slightly coarse, slightly hairy skin.

The testes produce sperms and testosterone, the hormone responsible for the sex drive. The testes can only produce sperms at a temperature of 35^0C, which is 2^0C cooler than the temperature inside our body. Each testis contains about 100 m long tiny coiled tube. Sperms are made inside these tubes from puberty until well into old age. When a man ejaculates, replacement sperms are made in these testes. These tubes also transport sperm-laden semen to vas deferens, which are muscular tubes. They are about 40 cm long. When a man ejaculates, sperms are squeezed through these tubes and out of the penis.

About a teaspoonful of semen that comes out, carries almost 400 million sperms. Nature makes sure that atleast one sperm reaches the egg.

Myths about the Testicles

Many men assume that the size of testicles influences sexual power and performance. Normal testicles do not depend upon size or shape. Most men have two testicles but some men have one non-descended testicle and they are able to function perfectly well. Sex drive is mainly influenced by thought patterns and not by the anatomical shape of any organ. Both testicles are never the same. Mostly one hangs lower than the other.

Being Normal

Most people have doubts about themselves in one way or another. If you think you are not normal, your body will not function normally. In 99% of cases, when people believe that something is wrong with them, it is a fact that their problem is psychological rather than physical. In sexual matters we seem to be obsessed with being normal.

A person may be a rich man or may be a distin-guished leader—but still feel inadequate in a simple act of sex that is common for animals and birds. This difference is due to negative preconditioning, concerning our normally based expectations of family and society.

Other Factors

80% of men have erection problems periodically. It is normal.

20% of men are bothered about premature ejaculation, due to lack of control.

10% of men have difficulty reaching orgasm and ejaculating semen.

If a man is able to satisfy the woman of his choice in any way that they mutually decide, he can consider himself normal.

Semen is the Seed of the Man

Earth is the essence of the elements,
Water is the essence of the earth,
Plants are the essence of the water,
Flowers are the essence of plants,
Fruits are the essence of flowers,
Man is the essence of the fruits,
Semen is the seed of the man.

(From *Udgith* in the Chandogya Upanishad)

Semen

Semen is a milky, sticky liquid. It is made of **Seminal Fluid,** released from the **Prostate Gland,** and **Seminal Vesicles.** It contains millions of sperms. About a teaspoonful of semen contains about 400 million sperms. As semen contains sperms, so, a woman can get pregnant if she has unprotected sexual intercourse with a man. During puberty some boys wake up at night to find semen coming out of their penis. Or boys wake up in the morning and find semen on their pyjamas or sheets. This means that they have had a *nocturnal emission* (wet dream).

Semen Myths

Throughout the world many fictitious beliefs and superstitions are prevailing concerning semen. Hindu religious leaders preach that the semen is the basis of health, strength and life, therefore, semen should be preserved and conserved through abstinence. Masturbation and nocturnal emissions are very harmful hence these should be avoided. That is why *Brahamcharya* has found a prominent place in the Hindu religious thinking.

Hindu belief is based on this conception that after eating 32 kg of food 800 gm blood is formed and out of that blood only 20 gm semen is formed. That means, if you have wasted 20 gm semen through masturbation or nocturnal emission, you have wasted the benefits of 32 kg food.

Early Chinese also held that ejaculation diminished the male element and therefore reduced the man's strength and may even shorten his life. Therefore various methods were used to retain as much semen as possible even during intercourse.

In early Tantric and Taoist Treatises the use of various techniques are suggested to regulate and control the emission of semen, so that it may ascend and nourish the brain. For this purpose a number of breath and thought control methods are suggested.

Such religious thinking helps the quacks to dupe the people of their hard earned money.

Role of the Scrotum and Testes in Producing Semen

The scrotum is a loose pouch of wrinkled darkish skin in which two testes of oval bodies are enclosed. The left testicle is slightly lower of the two and the whole structure is asymmetrical. In normal proportion the centre of the scrotum should reach lower down than the tip of the slack penis. There is no fatty layer. There are involuntary muscular tissues under the skin which contract in response to various stimuli. For instance, if they get too hot, the scrotum drops slightly so that the testes can cool down.

The scrotum is divided by a partition, in which the muscles are joined together and each division contains one testicle and one epididymis. Epididymis are two thin coiled tubules, which store the sperms that have been made in the testes. Sperms are formed in the testicles.

The mature testicle is 4 to 4½ cm long; at the utmost it does not exceed 5 cm. It is 2 to 3 cm broad and weighs between 15 to 26 gm.

The testicles are the parts of male reproductive system. The testicle on the left side is larger than the one on the right side. The two male testes hang down behind the penis. The nerves and blood-vessels enter the organs from behind. Besides this each testicle is joined and clasped from the back by the epididymis—an oval pad cushion. The head of the epididymis is fastened to the upper pole or extremity of the testicle and the two structures are closely interconnected.

The testicles are divided internally by a regular pattern of partitions into paramidical cups or cells. In each of these is a cluster of very minute curved and intertwined tubules, in which the spermatozoa, or sperm cells are formed. The testes produce the male sex hormone, *testosterone* which causes the changes in the body during puberty.

Hanging Scrotum

The reason why scrotum hang outside the body is that sperms are best produced at one or two degrees lower than the normal body temperature. The testes can only produce sperm at a temperature of 35 C, which is 2 degrees cooler than the temperature inside the body. If it is cooler outside, the skin of the scrotum shrinks, drawing the testes up towards the body for warmth. If they get too hot, the scrotum drops slightly so that the testes can cool down.

Sperm Cells

The production of sperm cells goes on in man from puberty to advanced old age at the rate of 500 million a day during peak production. The cells are termed seminal cells. A sperm looks a bit like a tadpole with a head, neck and a tail. The head transmits the qualities of genus and individual. The neck acts as oar to sweep the sperm forwards. These sperms come into motion when they are blended with a liquid secretion of the vesicles and prostate gland but in the testicles they remain motionless.

Only 200 to 300 million sperms are ejaculated at any one time. In fact, up to 100 million sperms can mature in just 24 hours.

Sperms Reach their Destination

Apart from the independent motion of the individual sperm cells, they are also driven forward and onward in the testicles by the accumulation of secretion, and gradual muscular apparatus of these ducts. They cover the last stage through the urethra with lightning speed and impetus in the ejaculation. If a man is having unprotected sexual intercourse with a woman and his penis is inside her vagina when he ejaculates, the sperm can swim through the woman's cervix into her uterus and travel up her fallopian tubes. If a single sperm meets a mature ovum here and joins with it, conception takes place.

Out of 200 to 500 million sperms that enter the vagina at the time of coitus only one is fortunate enough to enter the ovum. Others are expelled out by the vaginal secretions, which are too acidic to suit them as a medium. But the slight acidity of the vaginal secretions, at certain period of the cycle, and the distinctly alkaline spermatic fluid of uterine and tubular secretions, on the other hand, are very congenial to the sperms.

A man produces as much sperms as are needed. If he is not ejaculating due to masturbation or sexual intercourse, the production of the sperms slows down.

Function of the Prostate Gland

The prostate gland is a part of reproductive system. It surrounds the male urethra and is about the size of a golf ball.

During the spasmodic contractions or convulsion at the moment of sexual intercourse, this powerful muscular apparatus is able to squeeze and force the secretions it contains into the urethra. The ducts in which these secretions are formed are about thirty in number, and open-close together at the same place, in the urethral wall where the two seminal ducts also join the urethra.

The specific secretion of the prostate gland forms a milky-white, thin alkaline fluid containing sperms. These prostatic secretions are forced into the Urethra together with the sperm secretions from the testicles. Prostate secretion forms a large proportion of the ejaculate or discharge. Their alkalinity preserves the sperms and stimulates their mobility.

The length of the spermatic cord is about 45 cm. This length makes it a much more effective suction pump for the testicular products. This length also makes it able to contain a large amount of such secretions, so that throughout it may serve as a **reservoir**, as well as a conduit or duct. In the reservoir there are compartments in which the seminal fluid from the epididymis collects. Main storage of the semen takes place in the reservoir. When these are overfull the vesicles act as safety valves and extra containers.

The vesicular product is a tough, yellowish and sticky substance which gets mixed up in the seminal fluid.

Ejaculation

When the accumulated tension as a result of brimming seminal fluid in the reservoir and vesicles—has passed a certain limit, the involuntary muscles of these organs contract automatically in strong spasms. Then drive their fluid contents in tiny columns of spray against the anterior urethral wall. At the same time the prostatic muscles contract, and project the special secretions of the prostate gland into the urethra. It is a reflex action produced during copulation or masturbation and the sensation associated with it is also called **orgasm**.

Urethral Crest

It is not possible for the seminal fluid to flow away inwards in the direction of the bladder. And simultaneously it becomes impossible for the urine to pass with and get mixed into the semen, so long as the penis is in erection. The urethral crest makes it impossible to pass water or urine.

Penis after Ejaculation

After ejaculation, blood flows from the spongy tissue of the penis at a faster rate than fresh arterial blood flown in until the penis is flaccid again. Further stimulation persists and causes a renewal of the process once again.

Empty Reservoir and Vesicles

It is difficult to tell whether reservoirs and vesicles become entirely empty after ejaculation. But we find that it is possible to repeat coitus almost at once, so, we can assume that only a partial emptying of these organs takes place.

It is also true that complete or partial discharge is a matter of individual's particular way of thinking. That is why one man can only have coitus once on each occasion, and another several times in rapid succession.

But only a thin fluid is finally discharged which contains mostly prostatic secretion but no sperms or at most very few. For example, animals like cattle, sheeps and stallions etc. have reservoirs like man and so they perform coitus very quickly. However dogs and cats have no reservoirs and they are compelled to depend on vas deferens for their supply in coitus and hence take comparatively longer time.

Emmission of Sperms

In one ejaculation between 5 and 10 ml of semen is discharged containing about 60 million spermatozoa. When emission occurs in rapid succession, both quantity and quality diminish.

Longevity of Sperms

Once sperms have become fully developed at the man's reproductive organs, their life-span depends on where they happen to be. Mature sperms can be stored in the seminal vesicles for several weeks before they are reabsorbed as waste by the body. The ideal condition for the survival of sperm is a moist, warm, alkaline environment—such as found within the uterus. Here after intercourse, sperms can live for up to three days. Before ejaculation sperm's longevity can be measured in weeks and months.

Length of the Tube that Produces Sperms

Each testis contains about 100 metre of thread-like tubes in which sperms are made and transported to vas deferens.

Sperm Duct

Vas deferens is one of the two muscular tubes that join the testes to the ejaculatory duct via prostate gland. It carries spermatozoa to the urethra on ejaculation aided by contraction of its muscular wall.

Odour in the Semen

The prostate fluid which gets mixed in the semen cuases odour. This odour does not come from testicular secretion.

Composition of Man's Semen

The average one teaspoonful of semen contains, along with protein in the sperm, the sugar fructose, ascorbic acid, small amount of zinc and traces of cholesterol. It has calorific value of a raw carrot.

Swallowing Semen

Swallowing semen is absolutely harmless and might even have some nutritional value. But due to childhood taboos, many people are afraid of their natural secretion.

❑❑

Semen Related Problems

Masturbation

Sexual pleasure by stimulating the genitals, especially by hand, is called masturbation. Penis and clitoris are the special organs for masturbation. The act is usually accompanied by sexual fantasies and may involve the use of mechanical device such as a *vibrator*.

Masturbating can give good feeling and it can make one sexually excited enough to have an orgasm. Various surveys show that more than 90% of males and 80% of females use this technique of self arousal.

Myths Associated with Masturbation

Many myths are associated with masturbation. These are scaring the people for generations. There are lots of stories about terrible things that happen to people who masturbate—they go mad, go blind, can not have babies etc. These are not true. Masturbating can not do any harm and there is no need to feel guilty or scared about it. Some people do not want to masturbate because their religion or morals say that it is wrong.

Ways of Masturbation

There are different ways of masturbating. Men often hold the shaft of their penis in their hand and move their hand rhythmically up and down. Women may use their fingers or hand to rub their clitoris. Some masturbate their sexual partners by doing this for them.

Masturbation should not be thought as second best. The experience is a different one from sex with a partner. It does not involve the pleasures of sharing and giving, but it can be a useful way of relieving sexual tension.

Masturbation is not Harmful

Remember that masturbation can't do any harm and there is no need to feel guilty or scared about it. The belief that masturbating a great deal as youth could cause depletion of a man's semen supply late in life is erroneous. The male body continues to form semen even as mere secretions from the prostate and other glands without spermatozoa throughout life.

The only thing about masturbation which is in anyway damaging or bad is other people's negative attitude to it, which may harm and may induce guilt feelings in young people for no good reason.

Nocturnal Emission

Nocturnal emission is also called **wet dreams**. When semen leaks out of an adolescent boy's penis while he is asleep, it is called nocturnal emission. Nocturnal emission happens while people are dreaming, even if they are not dreaming about sex.

Orgasm during sleep are much common in men and women, typically starting in puberty and most frequent during adolescence. They may continue for many years into adulthood. It is more common in single men. It seems to be related to a man's general level of sexuality. Many married men also have wet dreams. These usually cease when a man reaches his fifties. Women can also have nocturnal orgasm with profuse sweating of the vagina. The contents of the dreams that accompany nocturnal arousal are usually erotic.

Involuntry seminal losses to which young men who are sexually abstinent are peculiarly liable owing to the accumulation of sperm. It can take place every fortnight, or three weeks and sometimes after every eight days. In later years they occur less often. The tension in the vesicles and reservoirs causes the motor reflexes of erection and emission, and that the dream passes through the mind concurrently. The local tension causes the dream and the dream causes the ejaculation. It is purely a physical example of the urge to relieve tension or urge of sexual evacuation.

Since the testes and seminal vesicles are always secreting and manufacturing semen, sometimes the vesicles are filled to capacity and the nature empties them in the form of nocturnal emission.

Nocturnal Emission is not Harmful

Nocturnal emission is not harmful in any way. In fact they are a sign that your reproductive organs are developing. They can happen quite often, during puberty. But don't worry if you don't have them. That is normal. Wet dreams are also a sign that you are normal.

Wet dreams are natural and harmless occurrence to be expected in most normal men between the age of fourteen and forty. They are a sign that your reproductive organs are developing normally. Even their absence does not necessarily indicate any abnormality.

Quacks Dupe the People

Quacks dupe the people by befooling them on the basis of baseless canards told by the religious leaders. Then they prescribe many types of prescriptions and create a sense of fear in them banking upon their ignorance. Millions of people are being fleeced every year in the name of nocturnal emission.

Premature Ejaculation

When a man ejaculates sooner than he expects to or wants to, it is called premature ejaculation. It has been established by research that anxiety about performance often causes premature ejaculation, as well as erectile failure. More than 80% of normal men experience this sexual difficulty at some point in their relationship. Without proper knowledge people can remain hung-over with subconscious fear of wrong doing even when they are enjoying in a mutually shared experience during marriage.

Such methods as the squeeze and stop start techniques are frequently effective in treating this condition. The intensity of ejaculation and orgasm are influenced by a number of factors, such as the degree of sexual excitement and the age and health of the individual.

In the past the concept of premature ejaculation was unknown. Indeed from the women's point of view, the sooner ejaculation occurred the better, since coitus was something to be endured rather than enjoyed.

Erections

When any person is sexually aroused, mental signals cause the valves of each penile reservoir to expand allowing blood circulation to pour into these swollen chambers. The chambers are fixed in place by connective, sponge-like tissue and as they swell by means of pressure from inside, the penis becomes erect and hard. Pressure detectors regulate the amount of circulation, and balance the erection, and degree of hardness. Afterwards when that person has ejaculated, the muscle relaxes. The blood flow returns to normal and the penis goes limp.

But erections can happen at other times too. One may find his penis slightly erect when he wake up in the morning. This is often because the bladder is full and is putting pressure on the penis. When urine is passed the erection goes away. The time taken by a male to get an erection from the start of sexual stimulation can be as low as 15 seconds in a young person and may take longer as a person grows older.

Erections Sabotaged

Research findings show that when any man tries to perform under negative circumstances, erection problem arises. The emotional pressure from within, causes his muscles to tighten their grip on the blood vessels that pass into the genital areas. This mind to body reflex interferes with normal function because erection can only take place when there is sufficient blood flowing into the arteries. The engorgement by the inflow of blood fluid is nature's means of maintaining rigidity.

When there is a conditioned pattern blocking impulses to the penis a sort of resistant armor is built up in that area. As the sphincter-muscles lock, the normal flow of circulation is cut off. Stress is at the root of most male impotence. Guilt and sex are antagonistic bedfellows.

Role of a Woman in the Erection

Many men believe that the woman is responsible for the state of erection. The truth, however, is that we are each responsible for our own sexual performance. Virility is always inner directed and self projected. The part that the woman plays depends on how much she cares about the man and how well the two people trust each other.

Retarded Ejaculation

Retarded ejaculation is caused due to emotional factors such as anxiety or insecurity, or aging. It may also be achieved by training in self-control as a means of extending the pleasure of intercourse.

Erectile Dysfunction

Inability of a male to achieve penile erection is called erectile dysfunction. The causes may be physical or psychic. If any man experiences an erection while sleeping but is unable to achieve an erection as a part of normal sexual activity, the cause is assumed to be psychic.

Physical causes may include low testostrone levels, which can be caused in turn by a disorder of the hypothalamus or pituitary glands, alcoholism, drug abuse, diabetes, mellitus, syphilis, multiple sclerosis, stroke, and prostatectomy also are among possible physical causes of erectile dysfunction. Nearly any drug that affects the autonomic nervous system may also affect sexual functioning.

Depression, sexual guilt and fear of intimacy are common psychic reasons. In many cases a single episode of erectile dysfunction may result in a fear of failure and mental attitude in which anxiety about a possible repetition of the episode becomes the psychic cause for erectile dysfunction.

Controlling Ejaculation

Ejaculation can be controlled by distracting one's thinking about another subject or by muscular relaxation. It may be done by slowing or ceasing pelvic thrusts. Squeeze techniques are also useful.

Tantric techniques advocate closing the eyes, opening the eyes wide, holding the breath, gnashing the teeth, and firmly pressing the area between the scrotum and anus, because the semen duct is located there.

❏❏

Female Sex Organs

Uterus

Uterus is a part of the female reproductive system. It is also called womb. It is a hollow muscular organ with thick walls located in the pelvic region of the female, the structure in which a fertilized ovum is nurtured into a viable individual. In a non-pregnant woman the uterus is a small pear shaped organ about 7 cm in length which protrudes at the cervical end into the vault of the vagina. Two fallopian tubes, or oviducts are attached to the uterus at both sides less than 2.5 cm from the top or fundus. The portion below the level of the tubes is the body of the uterus. All girls are born with a uterus.

Each month as part of the menstrual cycle, the lining of the uterus thickens in case an ovum is fertilized by a sperm. If the ovum is not fertilized, the thickened endometrium breaks down and pass out of the girl's or woman's vagina as her menstrual period. When the oavum is fertilized and the woman is pregnant, the uterus contains the unborn baby. It has to stretch a lot to make room for the baby to grow. By the time the baby is ready to be born, the uterus may be more than 50 cm long from top to bottom. During labour, muscles in the uterus tighten and relax in order to pull the cervix open so that the baby can pass out of the uterus. After the baby is born, the uterus starts to return to its normal size.

Female Sex Organs / 31

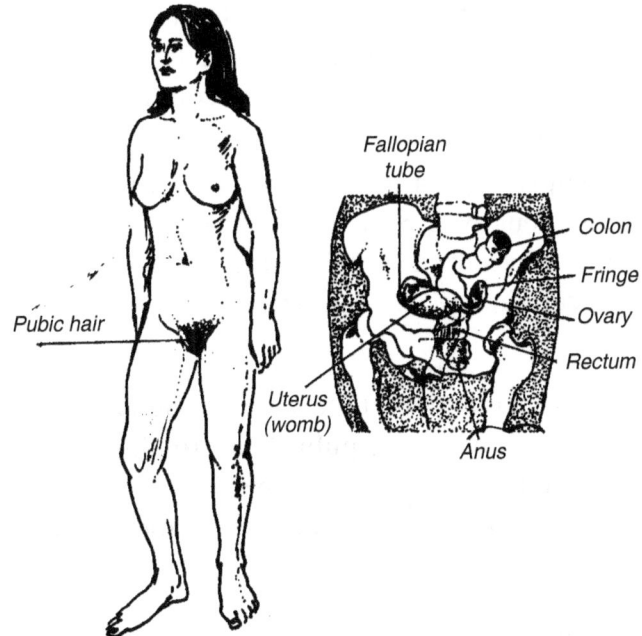

Female reproductive system

Vagina

Vagina is also a part of the female reproductive system. The vagina is a muscular tube inside a woman's body which connects her uterus to the outside of her body. It is about 10 cm long. The walls of the vagina are made up of soft folds of skin. The vagina is located anatomically between the bladder and the rectum and is supported by ligaments and muscles of the pelvic floor. Its walls are formed by an internal mucous membrane lining and a muscular coat, with an erectile tissue between them.

The main functions of the vagina are to provide passageway for spermatozoa from the penis to reach uterus. It is also an outlet for the menstrual flow from the uterus, and a birth canal for the foetus. The vaginal lining responds to stimulation by the female sex hormones

Oestrogen and **Progesterone**. This lining is continuous with uterus but it is not smooth surface. It is marked with furrows and ridges. These are called columns of vagina. The inside of the vagina can be dry or wet.

The empty vagina in a state of sexual response has an average length of 8 to 10 cm. At the time of coitus, penetration does not take place upto the root. This only occurs in certain special positions.

Vulva

Vulva is the name given to a woman's outer sex organ. After puberty it will have pubic hair growing there. The labia majora, the labia minora, the clitoris, the vestibules or opening of the vagina are the parts of the vulva.

Clitoris

It is the most sensitive part of the female genitals. The clitoris is where the inner labia meets at the front of the vulva. Only the tip of the clitoris is visible, and is covered by a hood or fold of skin.

The clitoris is full of nerve endings and when it is stimulated it becomes stiff like an erect penis and pokes out of its hood. Stimulating the clitoris helps many women to have an orgasm. The clitoris is, in fact, the **power house** of a woman's sexual feelings. It does not play any part in reproduction except to make sex play more pleasurable.

Like the penis, it has a suspensory ligament and two small muscles, which during sexual arousal are engorged by blood and become fuller and firmer. When this happens, the hood pulls back and exposes the delicate tip. But at the peak of excitement it shrinks back into its hood again. The clitoris may be stimulated directly by stroking the shaft slowly and gently to begin with and then faster and with a firm touch as excitement mounts.

During intercourse the pressure of the man's pubic bone against the clitoris may be sufficient stimulation for some women. For others the tugging action of the penis on the whole vulval area does the trick. But a large number of women need direct and continuous stimulation of the clitoris by hand at the time of penetration in order to reach orgasm. Typically, women like clitoral stimulation to be part of a total involvement and not to be seen like an obligation. It should be slow and soft at first, gradually building more pressure and speed. A technique frequently preferred is that stimulation should start with whole hand massage and then use only one or two fingers.

Labia

The word labia means lips. There are two types of labia—the outer labia and the inner labia.

The Outer Labia—These are also called labia majora. They are two pieces of thick skin that surround the vaginal orifice. These are shaped like a pair of lips and they consist of longitudinal folds of tissue that extend downwards and backwards from the mons pubis, enclosing the labia minora, the vagina, the urethra and the clitoris. The labia majora becomes wider and engorged with blood during sexual excitement. Pubic hair grows over the outer labia of the girls who have reached puberty. The outer labia are generally closed so that they can protect the more delicate parts underneath them such as the Vagina and the Clitoris.

The Inner Labia—The inner labia are also called labia minora. These are thinner than the outer labia and they can be seen when the outer labia are parted. They are sensitive to touch. As in the case of the labia majora, they also swell during sexual excitements. They come together in the prepuce of the clitoris at the upper end and in the hymen at the lower end.

Pubic Hair

Hair growth in the pubic region is one of the first signs of puberty. On the onset of puberty a patch of hair appears just above the genitals in a male and a female. The hair may vary in density, size and colour from person to person. This is considered to be a secondary sex characteristic. Even the sight of pubic hair is exciting to most men and some women.

Hymen

It is a very thin layer or membrane of skin which covers part of the vaginal opening. Every girl's hymen is different. Some women have hymens which look complete but which contain enough tiny holes to let menstrual blood flow through, when they have their menstrual period.

This delicate membrane stretches over the entrance of the vagina closing it partially. Many women have large opening in the hymen and some have no hymen at all.

Some religious and cultural groups expect a woman to have a complete hymen when she gets married. This is because one way in which a hymen is broken is through intercourse. If her hymen is broken, she is not considered as virgin. But this conception is not in conformity with fact.

For instance, those girls who ride a horse or a bike or do a lot of sports, gym or dancing, the hymen may get ruptured. By using a tampon in the vagina also hymen can be broken.

During the first act of intercourse, the hymen is normally torn, or atleast perforated, in two places on right and left. This penetration is accompanied by a slight loss of blood. It is almost always painful to a greater or lesser

Female Sex Organs / 35

degree. In women over 30 years of age it is hard and tough and offers considerable difficulties in coitus.

Various cultures foster the myth that all first instances of hymenal penetration are painful and show bleeding. To accommodate these expectations, women often feign pain and discomfort and ensure the presence of blood stains. A woman or her mother may see to it that some blood stains are visible.

Perineum

The area between a woman's labia and her anus is called perineum. When a woman has a baby, her perineum has to stretch until it is very thin. It might even tear or have to be cut to let the baby through. However, in the case of a man the region between the anus and scrotum is called Perinial. It is through this area that any treatment or diagnosis of the prostate is carried out.

Cervix

Cervix is the neck of the uterus and a passageway between the uterine cavity and the vagina. In a woman who has never been pregnant, the cervix is almost conical in shape. It protrudes from the uterus into the vault of the vagina. It is closed during pregnancy to contain the foetus but opens during **labour** so that the baby can leave the uterus and be pushed out through the vagina.

Fallopian Tube

There are two fallopian tubes or oviducts. They are muscular tubes, one on each side of the uterus. Every month as part of the menstrual cycle, an ovum is released by one ovary into the fallopian tube nearest to it. If a woman has sexual intercourse with a man around this time, the ovum may be fertilized by a sperm in the fallopian tube. As the ovum moves through the fallopian tube, it is most likely to encounter spermatozoa about halfway along the route to the uterus, the usual site of fertilization. However, any obstruction or lesion in fallopian tubes can be a reason of sterility.

Fimbria

The outer ends of the fallopian tubes are called fimbria. When ovulation takes place and an ovum is released, the fimbria sweep the ovum into the fallopian tube.

Ovary

Ovary is the part of female reproductive system. Women have two ovaries, one on each side of the uterus. They are attached to the uterus by fibres. They are oval in shape and about 4 cm long and 1 cm wide. In girls who have reached puberty, the ovaries take it in turns to release an ovum each month and to produce female sex hormones **Oestrogen** and **Progesterone** which are responsible for some of the changes which take place during the menstrual cycle. During puberty these hormones help reproductive organs grow and develop. The ovaries stop releasing ova after the menopause.

Ovum

The female sex cell or egg cell is called ovum. An ovum is so small that it can't be seen without a microscope. The ovum travels down the fallopian tube and if it meets a man's sperm, it is fertilized and it lodges itself in the woman's uterus and starts to develop into a baby. If it is not fertilized, it passes out of the woman's vagina in her vaginal fluid. Girls are born with 4 lakhs ovas stored in their ovaries. But only about 300 to 500 are released during a woman's fertile years between puberty and the menopause. The remaining disintegrate.

❑❑

Puberty

Puberty is that point in human development when the reproductive organs start working, girls ovulate for the first time and boys can ejaculate. Secondary sex characteristics such as pubic and facial hair, enlarged breasts and genitals, begin to appear. Feelings and emotions also change during puberty.

Action of Hormones

Puberty occurs due to the action of the hormones. It starts in the brain where the hypothalamus triggers the pituitary gland to start to produce hormones. These hormones cause changes in the ovaries in girls and testes in boys.

In girls, the ovaries start to release an ovum each month causing menstruation. They also produce female sex hormones Oestrogen and Progesterone.

In the boys, the testes start to produce sperm. They also produce the male sex hormone Testosterone. These hormones help the reproductive organs and genitals to continue to develop.

The changing level of hormones also cause the appearance of so-called secondary features such as pubic and facial hair, enlarged breasts and genitals.

Biological Clock

Everyone has their own biological clock. All the changes which take place during puberty, including the growth of body hair, are caused by the release of hormones. This

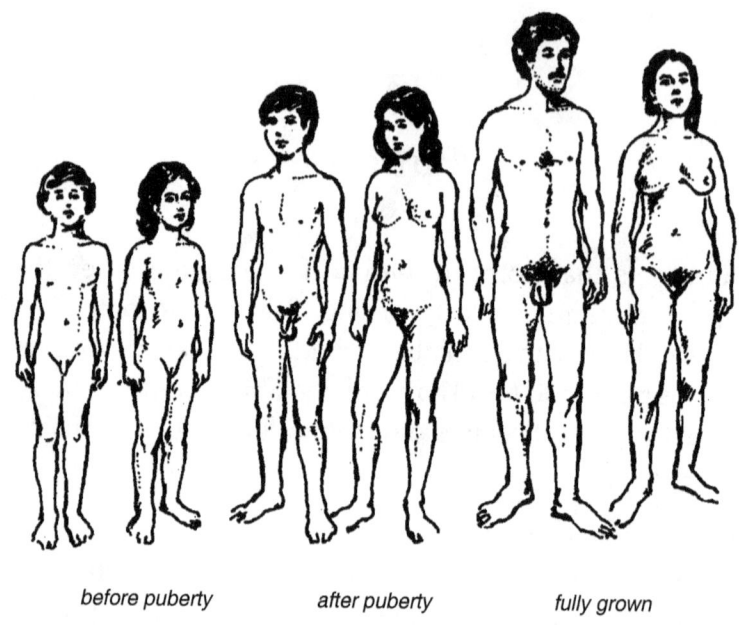

before puberty   *after puberty*   *fully grown*

Childhood to adolescence

takes place at different times and rates for each individual. The changes occur more quickly for some and even in a different order.

Puberism

This term is referred to the retarded development of secondary sexual characteristics such as breasts or beard because of undersecretion of sex hormones. In many cases development may be so retarded that the individual gives the appearance of an eternal adolescent.

Changes in Girls During Puberty

Girls grow a lot over a short period of time during puberty when the pituitary gland sends growth hormones around the body, but it varies from person to person. The breasts develop. Around the genitals pubic hair grows. Hair also grows under the arms and legs. Girls start to have periods at about 13 years of age. They sweat more especially around the genitals and under arms. Face changes shape. The voice gets a bit deeper, muscles get bigger and change shape. The uterus become pear shaped. Clitoris grows and becomes more sensitive.

Changes in Boys During Puberty

A number of changes take place in boys. The testes get bigger and start to produce sperm. Scrotum gets darker and changes texture. Penis grows and becomes more sensitive. Now boys have more and more erections. They have wet dreams. Pubic hair grows around genital and may also have a line of hair growing from genital area to navel. Hair also grows under arms and on face. More body hair grows. Voice breaks wavering between high and low notes. Boys sweat more especially around their genitals and under their arms. Muscles get bigger and change shape.

All these changes don't happen overnight. A common age for girls to start puberty is 11 and for boys it is 13. But it differs from person to person.

After puberty the adolescence starts when dependence and immaturity gradually give way to independence and maturity. It is a time of emotional stress and strain, identity crisis, change in sexual characteristics and body image, experimentation with different sex roles and different self concepts and high sex interest. It is time of life when a girl changes into a young woman and a boy change into a young man.

❏❏

Menstruation and Menopause

Menstruation

The monthly discharge of blood and tissue from the uterus of a woman is called menstruation. It is absolutely normal and healthy and not a sign that something is wrong. A girl begins to menstruate when she begins pubery. This can be any time between the age of 9 and 18. The average age is about 13. The beginning of menstruation is determined by the release of hormones according to the particular girl's own internal timetable, regardless of when other girls start.

Menstruation generally happens every month between puberty and menopause but not while the woman is pregnant or breast feeding.

Menstruation occurs because sex hormones make the **Endometrium** grow thicker and get soft and spongy, ready to receive, a fertilized ovum. If no ovum is fertilized, the thickened endometrium is not needed, so it breaks away from the uterus and passes out of the vagina together with a little blood during menstrual period. It is also called menses or monthly period.

Endometrium is a specialised form of mucous membrane that lines the uterus. It is divided into two main types of tissue. One is the *pars functionalis*, which is shed during menstruation, and the *pars basilis* which is not shed and serves as the base for the proliferation of cells for the layers of *pars functionalis* that develop during the next menstrual cycle.

Menstruating women need to use sanitary towels,

pads or tampons to soak up the menstrual flow. After menstruation, the endometrium starts to thicken again and the whole menstrual cycle repeats itself.

Many girls and women have no problems when they menstruate. But some get an ache or cramp-like pain in their lower abdomen before and during menstruation. Some girls and women also get sore breasts, have headache and feel tired, irritated or depressed before they menstruate. Some women and girls have the same problems everytime, whenever they have their menstrual period.

Premenstrual Tension

Some women have same problems every time they have their menstrual period. The problems usually start a week or two before menstruation. They vary from woman to woman but include things like depression, anxiety, mood swings, headaches, feeling dizzy, putting on weight, feeling bloated, sore breast, and a craving for starchy and sweet things. The problems usually go away after the menstrual period starts and then come back again before the next one starts.

When once you have started to menstruate regularly you will soon learn to recognise tell-tale signs in yourself which mean the next period is on its way.

Duration of Menstrual Period

A menstrual period usually lasts between two to eight days and happens once a month. Normal menstrual discharge lasts from 3 to 5 days. Average bleeding period is four days and the amount of blood discharged varies from one to five ounces.

If you have indulged in unprotected sexual intercourse

42 / Sex Problems

and your menstrual period stops, you might be pregnant and should see a doctor. About 50% women do not menstruate while they are nursing the baby at the breast.

Menstrual Cycle

A monthly process in which the female reproductive organs get ready for the possibility of pregnancy. The main events in the menstrual cycle are ovulation, the thickening of the endometrium and menstruation. The length of the menstrual cycle can be anything from 20 to 36 days. But the average cycle is about 28 days long. Over 70% of all

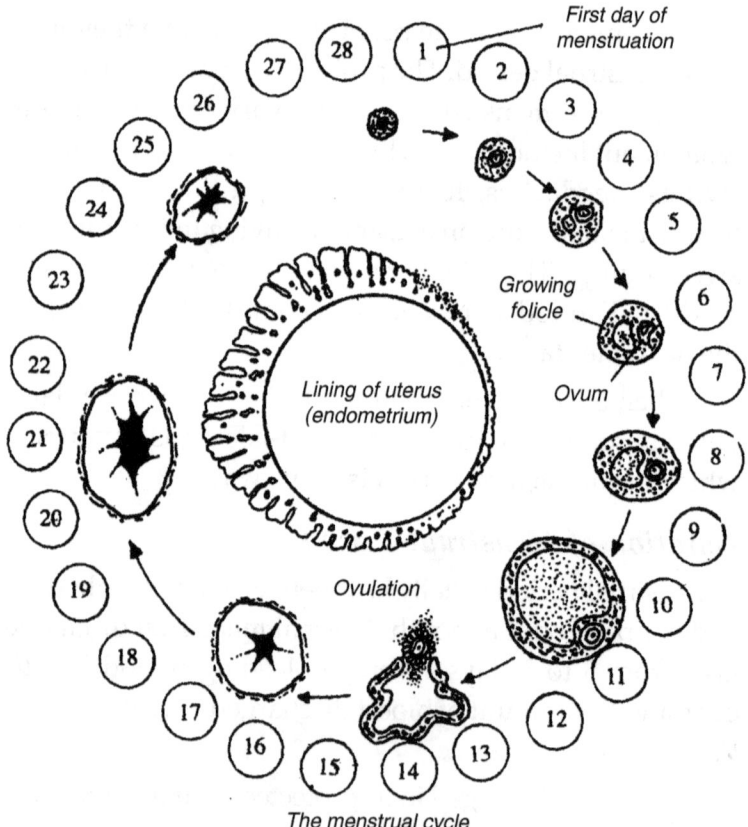

The menstrual cycle

Menstruation and Menopause / 43

women menstruate approximately every twenty eight days. Remaining 28% experience considerable variations from the average.

It is estimated that a woman who starts to menstruate at 13, stops at 50 and has two children could have more than 400 menstrual cycles in her life time. When girls start menstruating, their menstrual cycles are often not very regular. They may menstruate three or four times in the first year. A middle aged woman's menstrual cycle may also become irregular before the menopause.

Sudden shock, worry or great joy can affect the cycle and may make the menstrual period come late or early or prevent it altogether. These are called psychic impression and sensations. There are women who are regular to time. Others are never quite certain when to expect the period. Influence of climate, way of life, constitutional and hereditary tendencies may cause variations.

Myths Connected with the Menstruation

There are many myths attached to menstruation. There are many dos and don'ts to be followed during your menstrual period like you must not wash your hair or have a bath or play sports etc.

Some religious and cultural restrictions are also inposed during this period like the girls cannot enter the kitchen or do puja etc.

Sex During Menstruation

Excitement during the menstrual cycle is quite significant in women. Sometimes the desire for sex is quite high in some women during menstrual period. Modern medical researchers on behavioural sex have conclusively established that sexual intercourse performed during mentruation period is not harmful at all. If the partners do not mind the mess, they can merrily go ahead. Moreover, there is an added advantage, the chances of conception are negligible.

Still it is considered unhygienic in many communities to indulge in sex with a woman undergoing the menstruation period. Actually, it is more out of aesthetical consideration that such acts are avoided.

There is, however, no doubt that medically such acts are not forbidden but obviously they would cause much inconvenience to both. Medical theories apart, one can hardly enjoy the act during the menses. Therefore, sometimes a taboo would seem more rational than the rationality of medical theories.

Time to Exercise

This is particulary a good time to exercise, since moderate activity helps relieve cramps and the sensation of heaviness often experienced during a period. If you are bleeding a lot, it is a good idea to use a tampon and a sanitary towel for exta protection. You can carry on all your regular activities as normal.

Follicle

Follicle is a tiny ball of cells in a woman's ovary. A follicle contains an ovum. Follicles play an important part in a female's menstrual cycle. About every 28 days, between 10 and 20 follicles start to mature, producing the sex hormone *estrogen* as they do so. At the time of ovulation, one follicle bursts open and releases an ovum. Once it has released the ovum, it starts to produce another sex hormone *progesterone*. Oestrogen and progesterone prepare the endometrium to receive the nourished fertilized ovum. If the ovum is not fertilized, the ovum *corpus luteum* and endometrium start to break and menstruation takes place.

Follicle Stimulating Hormone

It is a hormone produced by the pituitary gland, in the girls who have reached puberty as well as in boys. Its function is to stimulate ovarian follicle growth in the female and spermatogenesis in the male. Production of the follicle stimulating hormone begins to increase significantly at puberty, and in the male it is believed to influence the growth of the seminiferous tubules of the testes. It helps the testes to produce sperm.

Menopause

The period during which menstruation ceases and the female reproductive cycle comes to an end is called menopause. But sexual desire and enjoyment are usually maintained and may actually increase when fear of pregnancy is no longer a concern.

Most women start the menopause when they are about 50 years old. But it can happen any time between the age of 40 and 55. A woman's menstrual period may be irregular for a year or two before they actually stop. Women going through the menopause often have hot flushes, night sweats and vaginal dryness. Emotions and personality are also affected during menopause and they may become irritable or depressed. Some women find the menopause hard to cope with as it affects their bodies and feelings. Other women are pleased to reach the menopause because it means no more menstrual periods and no more worries about getting pregnant.

Sexual Maturity in Women

Sexual maturity lasts longer in some women than in others. In 40% of women it ceases between forty-six and fifty years of age; in about 26% between forty-one and forty-five or more commonly before forty.

As a rule, sexual maturity ceases earlier in women who have not borne children than in those who have. A late child birth which occurs after forty years of age, postpones the menopause. The influence of race and climate also affect it.

Ceasation of this function affects all the activities of a woman. The cyclic ebb and flow of maturity ceases, and the vital processes remain at a continous level of a lesser degree of vigour and acuteness than the average of former years.

Effects of Menopause

One of the signs of changes in metabolism is frequently increased development of fat all over the body. There are palpitations, dizziness, vertigo, roaring in the ears and blackness before the eyes; all the signs of faintness.

Some women find the menopause hard to cope with because of the way it affects their bodies and feelings. Some other women are pleased to reach menopause because it means no more menstrual periods and no more worries about getting pregnant. Thus the mental balance forms a well merited compensation of nature for extremely high biological demands of women during sexual maturity.

❏❏

Pregnancy

Pregnancy refers to the time span between the conception of a foetus and the delivery of the child.

When a man and a woman have sexual intercourse, the man puts his erect penis into the woman's vagina. When he ejaculates, a small amount of semen containing upto 400 million tiny sperms shoot out at the end of his penis and into the woman's vagina. These sperms then swim through the woman's cervix into her uterus. Some get as far as the woman's fallopian tubes where they may meet a mature ovum on their way to the uterus.

Fertilization

Fertilization takes place if one sperm manages to get through the outer layer of the ovum and joins with the ovum to form a new cell called **zygote**. This new cell will eventually develop into a baby. The woman does not produce any ova while she is **pregnant**. So fertilization can not happen again until after she has had the baby.

Doctors and midwives do not count pregnancy from the day of fertilization but from the first day of a woman's last menstrual period. The pregnancy usually lasts for 40 weeks. But a pregnancy can be shorter or longer depending on the biological condition of the mother. The average pregnancy lasts 280 days or nine calendar months. Doctors divide pregnancy into three trimesters, each lasting for three months.

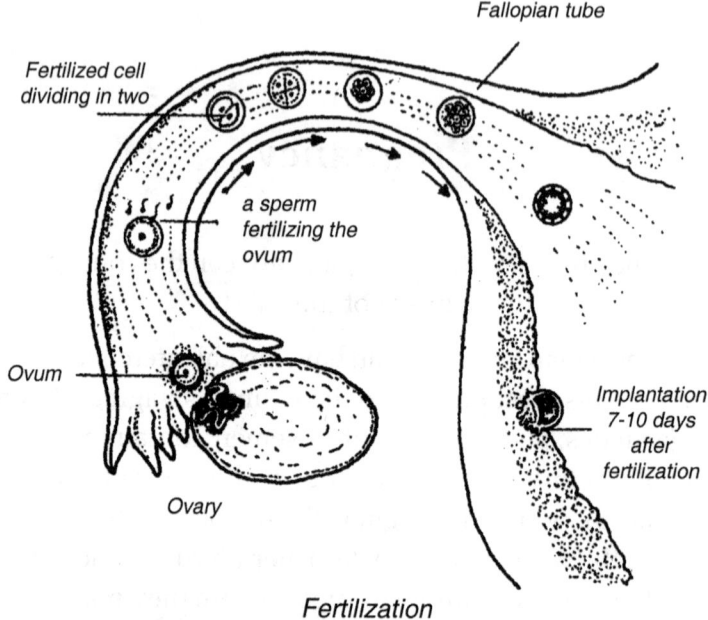

Fertilization

First Trimester

During the first trimester, the woman can feel very tired and may have morning sickness. While the baby is developing and growing inside her, her body too starts changing. Her breasts get larger. She probably has more vaginal discharge and needs to pass urine more often. She may also have a strange taste in her mouth and may have a craving for certain foods.

By the end of the first trimester, the foetus is fully formed and woman starts to bloom and feel much better. She may feel happy and excited about being pregnant. But most women have days when they worry or are fed up with being pregnant.

Second Trimester

The second trimester marks the woman's changing shape. In the fourth or fifth month, the foetus heart starts to beat

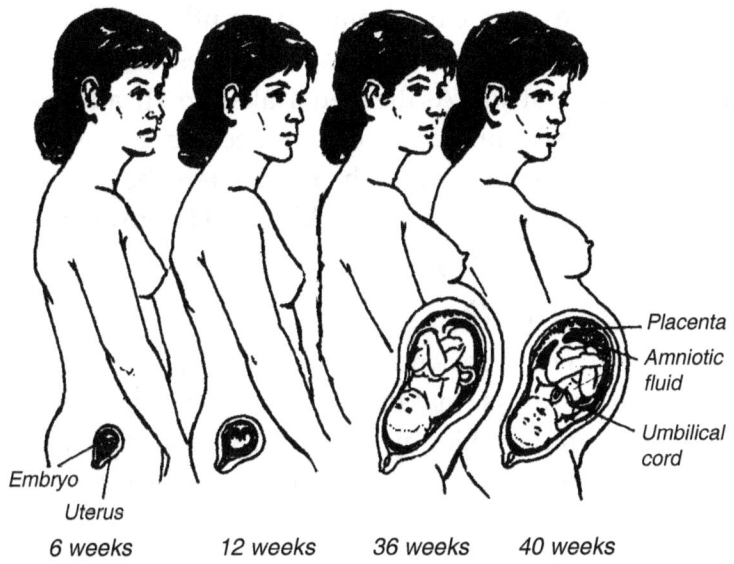

Changes in mother's figure during pregnancy

and it begins to move. All this confirms the reality of the pregnancy. Most women carry on a dialogue of sorts with the foetus, slowly making it a part of their life. Expectant parents accept the presence of the baby in the womb and give an affectionate name to it.

By the end of the second trimester, the foetus may weigh 2 lb but the mother may have gained 10 lb. Some women show patches of temporary skin discoloration on the face, stomach and breasts. A clear yellow secretion called colostrum may seep from the nipples. These changes are harmless but undue weight gain should be controlled.

Third Trimester

During the final trimester, the foetus continues to grow, gaining about one lb a week-during the last two or three weeks. By the eighth month, all the body systems of the foetus are well developed and it is ready for the precarious life outside the womb. The ninth month in the womb ensures extra strength and better resistence to the trauma of life outside. As the foetus takes up a head-down position in the womb, its movements become increasingly noticeable to the mother. As the head enters the pelvis, it pushes against the mother's bladder, making urination a more frequent necessity.

Preparing for Birth

As the foetus enlarges and moves down, the diaphragm is pushed upwards, making rib cage and breasts more protuberant and breathing more audible. As birth approaches, the foetus can be felt pushing down against the pelvis muscles and cervix. This is variously called engagement, lightening or dropping. Gradually the *cervix* (neck) or exit from the womb, becomes thinner. This process is known as effacement. The woman's pelvis now begins to relax.

This makes walking awkward and sometimes painful but it is a part of the preparation for birth and a sign that labour will soon begin.

Labour Pains

Labour is the passage of the foetus and placental tissues from the womb, via the vagina, to the outside. It is usually described as having three phases.

In the first phase of labour, the cervix, which is closed with a plug of mucus during pregnancy, opens up, strong muscular contractions of the uterus help this to happen, but it can still take between two and twelve hours for the cervix to stretch enough to let the baby out.

In the second phase, the baby passes out of the uterus and down the woman's vagina. The woman has to push hard with each contraction until the baby's head starts to come out through the vaginal opening.

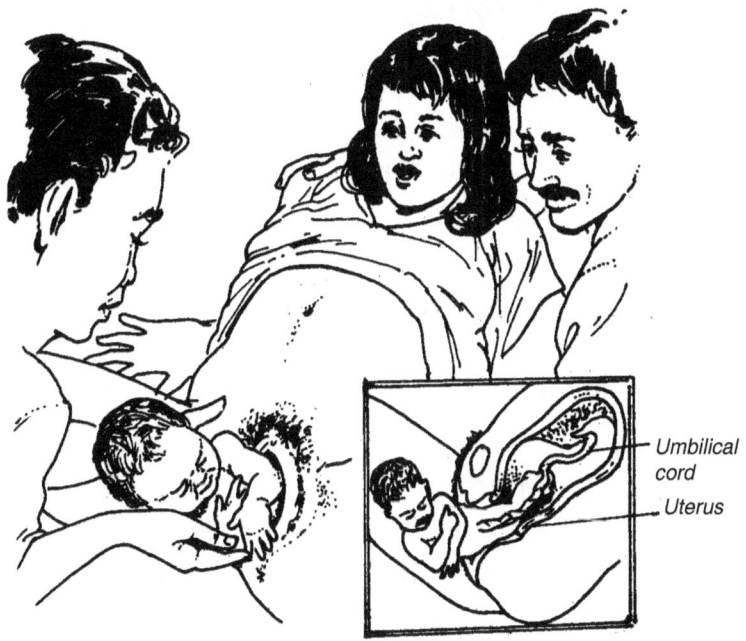

The third phase is the expulsion of the placenta and its associated membranes.

The process of labour is extremely variable from woman to woman, and even in the same woman first, second and third labours may be very different. First birth generally takes longer and is more painful than the subsequent ones.

Myths about Pregnancy

In many cultures great magical significance is given to the placenta and umbilical cord. They hide the after-birth placenta and umbilical cord in case it fell into the hands of evil wishers.

Pregnancy Test

It is a test to check if the woman is pregnant or not.

Pregnancy tests work by seeing if there is a certain hormone in urine. It is done two weeks after the first day of the missed menstrual period. If the test result is positive you are certainly pregnant. If the test result is negative and you still haven't had your period, a week later one more test should be done.

Say No to Drugs

Pregnant women are advised to use extreme caution in taking any drug during pregnancy because medical studies now indicate that many drugs, including alcohol, can cause birth defects.

Thalidomide Babies

In 1953, a tranquilizer was developed in Germany and was marketed as a safe sedative. It was named **Thalidomide**. In animal tests it was found that the drug had virtually no toxic effects in masses doses, and therefore would be a suitable substitute for barbituates because it would be virtually impossible for a patient to take a lethal overdose.

In 1960, it was discovered that pregnant women who took thalidomide were delivered of deformed children with a variety of defects. The most common birth defect was *phocomelia* - born with arms and legs that were extremely short or with parts missing.

In retrospective research, it was found that thousands of women with children so afflicted had taken doses of thalidomide during the fourth week of pregnancy, when the embryonic limb buds were forming. Those who took the drug on days when the eyes or ears were forming gave birth to infants with visual or hearing difficulties, Consequently Thalidomide was taken off the market.

Caesarian Section

The delivery of a baby through a surgical incision in the abdomen is called caesarian section. The purpose of the procedure is to preserve the life and health of both the mother and the child, particularly when delivery of a foetus through the vaginal birth canal is not possible. Caesarian delivery has traditionally been an emergency operation, but in recent years the procedure has become increasingly an elective procedure. The mother is given an **Epidural** block or anaesthetic so that she does not feel any pain.

A contributing factor to the increased popularity of caesarian delivery has been the development of more sophisticated foetal monitoring devices that indicate well in advance that a breech presentation or other type of vaginal or pelvic difficulty may threaten the welfare of the mother or child, or both.

Miscarriage

Miscarriage is the spontaneous expulsion of the foetus before it is able to survive outside the uterus—usually before the 28th week of pregnancy. If a woman has a miscarriage, her baby usually dies. Miscarriages occur in 10 to 15% of pregnancies, and in about 50% of cases, the foetus is found to be clearly defective.

It may happen if the woman's placenta is not working properly or if she has a weak cervix which opens too early. If a woman has a miscarriage, it does not mean she can't have another baby. Many women who have a miscarriage go on to have a successful pregnancy next time.

Premature Baby

A baby born before the 37th week of pregnancy is called premature baby. Generally pregnancy is expected to last for 40 weeks. Premature babies may need special medical care during the first few days after their birth, but they usually grow into normal, healthy babies.

Still Birth

When a baby is born dead, it is called still birth. Some babies also die shortly after they are born. Some of the factors that are commonly involved are immaturity of the foetus, syphilis, protracted labour, water in the lungs and strangulation by the umbilical cord.

Stone Baby

A foetus that dies within the uterus without being aborted and is instead preserved by a bone like layer of calcium salts is called a stone baby. The calcium shroud presumably develops to protect the mother from the toxic effects of the dead foetus. A stone baby may remain undetected in a uterus for many years.

Umbilical Cord

Umbilical Cord is the cord that connects the foetus with the placenta and provides a means for the flow of nutrients from the maternal blood supply to the foetus and for the removal of the products from foetal metabolism.

An unborn baby does not eat and breathe like we do. Instead, food and oxygen pass from the mother's blood through the placenta and down the umbilical cord to the baby. It is about 50 cm long and 2.5 cm thick. At birth this cord is clamped and cut. This does not hurt the baby or the mother. A little bit of cord is left attached to the baby. New skin forms under this bit of cord and after about a week the cord drops off on its own. It forms the navel of the baby.

Placenta

Placenta is an organ of pregnancy that is attached to the

inner wall of the uterus and is connected to the foetus by an umbilical cord. The blood vessels in the umbilical cord provide all the nutrients for the growth and maturation of the foetus and carry away the waste of its metabolism. It provides the unborn baby with the food and oxygen it needs to grow and develop. One side of the placenta is fixed to the wall of the mother's uterus. The umbilical cord comes out of the other side and goes into the unborn baby's navel. An unborn baby does not eat and breathe like we do. Food and oxygen pass from the mother's blood through the placenta and down the umbilical cord to the baby. Waste products from baby pass back through the cord and placenta and into the mother's blood.

Antibodies which help the baby fight infections once it is born can also pass through the placenta from the mother to the baby. So can harmful things like alcohol, drugs and nicotine from cigarette. That is why it is best for the pregnant woman not to smoke, drink alcohol or take drugs.

In a multiple pregnancy there may be more than one placenta. The uterus moves about one pint of blood per minute into the placenta and a slightly smaller amount returns during uterine relaxation. The foetus thus gains a small amount of blood materials in each exchange.

Women have been advised to use extreme caution in taking any drug during pregnancy because studies now indicate that many drugs including alcohol, can cause birth defects.

Sex of the Baby

To a biologist, a pregnancy is first a zygote, then an embryo, then a foetus and only after birth, a baby. But for the hopeful parents a pregnancy is a baby right from the start.

Every pregnant woman is viewed as a future mother. Studies reveal that for more than 50% of women pregnancy is unplanned. In our country this percentage is more than 90%. That is the reason why we are producing as many children in one year as the total population of Australia. Many women accept this fact fatalistically.

But more and more educated women are choosing to abort, and in many societies they are supported in their decision. Our Government is also encouraging birth control methods to control the growth of the population.

The unit of fertilization contributed by each parent are called **Gametes**. The male gametes are sperm produced by the testes and the female gametes are eggs, or ova produced by the ovaries.

The sex of the zygote is determined at the time of fertilization since all ova contain an X-sex chromosome. So, the male's sperm is the determining factor. If it too contains an X-chromosome, the zygote will be female (XX) but if it contains a Y-chromosome, the zygote will be male (XY).

Reason is not known, but though more male zygotes are produced than female, there are more deaths among infant males than among infant females.

The knowledge that it is the sperm of the male that determines sex is being widely disseminated in countries like China and India, where traditionally female babies have been looked on as worthless and wives brutally abused for producing them.

Various techniques are now available for determining the sex of the foetus.

Myths about the Desired Sex

Although there is no simple or reliable method of ensuring

that a baby is of the desired sex, yet folk nostrums and quack remedies abound in many societies and cultures because many people would like to choose the sex of their baby. In many cultures, boys are usually preferred to girls.

One such myth is having coitus in a certain position or at certain times of the menstrual cycle. Such myths are prevailing throughout the world.

One of the oldest notion is that one testicle contains sperm producing only girls, and the other holds sperm that produce only boys. But these are only myths holding no truth in them.

❏❏

Sexual Diseases

Sex is pleasant and rewarding for most of us. But for a sizeable minority of people sex has its darker side. There are a number of diseases, some causing several physical and mental distress, that are closely related to sexual behaviour. Many people react to this hard fact by refusing to think about the possibility of disease until they are personally infected or affected. But prevention is better than cure. Although not all sex related diseases can yet be cured, most can be controlled, and all are more likely to respond to treatment if detected early.

Sexually Transmitted Diseases

Sexually transmitted diseases are those diseases that are passed directly from one person to another through sexual contact. They include those ailments traditionally called **Veneral Diseases** or genito-urinary infections as well as many other.

You can never be sure without laboratory tests. There are many different types of STD, some of which affect both sexes, some only men, and some only women. No one knows when and where STDs started, but the diseases have been with us for a long time. The first symptoms such as itching, soreness, pain on urination are often similar, or there may be no symptoms that you can see or feel. If you notice any symptoms, or if you think you may have picked up an infection and you have had several sexual partners, go at once to your doctor or to a special clinic. Treatment and cure in the early stage is usually simple but putting off treatment can be fatal.

Here are some common STDs, their causes, symptoms and treatment:

1. Genital Herpes

Cause—A virus which you can catch by *having sex* with someone who has an active infection.

Symptoms
- Itching, tingling or aching in the *vulva, penis* or *testes*.
- Itching to followed by sores, usually on and around the *genital* area. Some women have sores on their *cervix* too but they cannot feel these. The sores change to watery blisters in a day or two and usually burst and heal themselves without treatment.

While you have the sores, you may:
- Feel pain when you pass *urine*.
- Feel as though you have got flu (headache, backache and high temperature).

Treatment—There is no cure for genital herpes but there are remedies to make you feel more comfortable if you have it. Your doctor or *Special Clinic* might be able to help.

2. Genital Warts

Cause—A virus which you can catch by *having sex* with someone who is infected.

Symptoms
- Fleshy growths or warts on the *genital* area. They may also grow in the *vagina, anus* or *cervix* where they cannot be easily seen.

Treatment—Sometimes a special ointment is painted on the warts to get rid of them. There may be a link between genital warts and *cervical cancer*. Women who have had genital warts or whose *sexual partners* have genital warts should have regular *cervical smear tests*. If you think you have genital warts you should go to your doctor or to a *Special Clinic*.

3. Gonorrhoea

Cause—A bacterium which you can get by *having sex* with an infected person.

Symptoms—60% of women and 10-15% of men who have gonorrhoea have no symptoms. Others have:
- Pain when passing *urine*.
- An unusual *discharge* from the *vagina* or a yellowish discharge from the *penis*.
- An itchy *anus* or a discharge form the anus.
- A sore throat if you have caught gonorrhoea through *oral sex*.

Women may also have:
- A fever or *'chill'*.
- Pain in the *abdomen*
- Painful *joints* (knees, wrists etc.).

Treatment—Antibiotics which you can get from your doctor or a *Special Clinic*. You need to have regular checkups after you have finished the antibiotics to make sure the infection has been cleared up.

4. NSU (Non-Specific Urethritis)

Cause—A bacterium which you can get by *having sex* with someone who is infected. Doctors do not always know which bacterium causes NSU that's why it is called 'non-specific'.

Symptoms—Urethritis means inflammation of the *urethra*.
- Pain when passing *urine*.
- *Discharge* from the *penis*.

Treatment—Antibiotics which you can get from your doctor or a *Special Clinic*.

5. Cystitis

Cause—Bacteria which you can get by *having sex*. But you can also get cystitis without *sexual contact*.

6. Pubic Lice

Cause—Small lice (insects) in the *pubic hair* which can be spread by close body contact during sex.

Symptoms
- Very itchy *genital* area.
- Small eggs or nits (empty egg cases attached to your *pubic hair*.

Treatment—A special lotion which you put on your *genital* area. You can get it from a *Special Clinic*. Ordinary washing with soap and water will not kill the lice or get rid of the nits.

7. Chlamydia

Cause—A bacterium which you can get by *having sex* with someone who is infected.

Symptoms

In Women:
- Pain or a burning feeling when they pass *urine*.
- A thin *vaginal discharge* and/or pain in the *abdomen* perhaps with a fever. (Many women have no symptoms until the infection has spread to the *fallopian tubes*).

In Men:
- A burning feeling when they pass *urine*.
- A *discharge* from the *penis*.

Treatment—Antibiotics from your doctor or a *Special Clinic*. In women, chlamydia can lead to *Pelvic Inflammatory Disease (PID)*. PID can make a woman *infertile*. So if you have had *sexual contact* with someone who has got chlamydia, you should go to your doctor or a *Special Clinic* straightaway.

8. Syphilis

Cause—A bacterium which you can get by *having sex* with an infected person. Syphilis is not very common these days.

Symptoms

Stage 1: 1-2 weeks after infection.
- A painless sore on or near the *vagina* or *penis*.

Stage 2: 2-6 weeks after infection
- A rash on the body.
- You feel as though you've got flu (headache, sore throat, fever).

Stage 3: Years after infection

Stage 3 is very rare because most people are cured before this stage.

Symptoms are:
- Permanent damage to the heart, brain and other *organs*.

Treatment—Can be cured with antibiotics which you can get from your doctor or a *Special Clinic*. You will need regular check-ups after you have finished the antibiotics to make sure the infection has been cleared up. Syphilis must be treated early. If it is left untreated, it can kill you.

9. Scabies

Cause—Scabies can be passed on through *sexual contact* with someone who is infected but this is rare.

Symptoms—The tiny creatures which burrow under the top layers of the skin make you itch very badly. The itching is often worse at night. You may have red raised bumps on the skin, particularly between fingers or under the breasts, around the waist and on genitals or buttocks.

Treatment—Can get rid of it by treating the whole body with a special lotion which could be purchased from the chemist. Some people also wash their bed-clothes, towels and flannels in very hot water to avoid getting scabies again, although the risk of infection in this way is very small.

10. Trichomoniasis

Cause—A tiny organism or *cell* which affects the *vagina* and *urethra*. You can get trichomoniasis by *having sex* with someone who is infected.

Symptoms
In Women:
- Yellow or white *discharge* from the *vagina* which is quite smelly.
- Itchy vaginal area.

In Men:
May have no symptoms so they may not know they have got it.

Treatment—Special tablets which you can get from your doctor or a *Special Clinic*.

11. Thrush

Cause—A yeast infection which you can get by *having sex* with someone who is infected. But you can also get thrush without *sexual contact*. It is caused by a yeast called *canadia albicans* which affects the vulva and vagina in women and may affect penis in men.

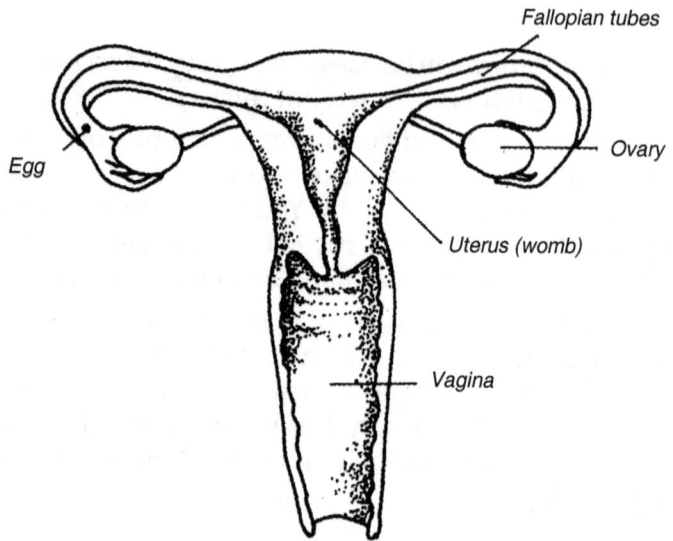

Symptoms—Signs for a woman that she has got thrush include itching around her vulva and a thick white discharge from her vagina. The vulva may also smell a little and it may hurt to pass urine. Signs for a man that he has got thrush include a sore and itchy penis.

Treatment—Women who think they have thrush can try treating themselves by putting a *tampon* dipped in plain yoghurt into their vagina. If this does not work, they should see their doctor. Doctor may prescribe *pessaries* and possibly a cream. Men are usually given a cream.

12. AIDS

AIDS stands for Acquired Immune Deficiency Syndrome, a condition where natural defences against infection are knocked out. This meaning that AIDS patients are likely to get infections which the body would normally fight off. In people with lowered resistance, these can prove fatal.

AIDS victims may develop certain kinds of cancer, as well as serious infections in the lungs, skin or digestive or central nervous system.

Cause—AIDS is caused by a virus known as HIV. When it gets into the blood stream, it may kill off certain white blood cells which normally act to fight off germs. This leaves the body open to infections of all kinds.

The two main ways in which the disease is passed on are—by direct sexual contact; and by getting infected blood into the blood stream. This deadly virus is also known to be transmitted from the mother to the unborn baby in the womb or at birth, or to a baby through the mother's milk.

Symptoms—A few of its symptoms are:

Swollen glands especially in the neck and armpits;

Profound fatigue, which lasts for several weeks.

Unexpected weight loss, fever and swelling at night, lasting for several weeks.

Diarrhoea which lasts for more than a week with no obvious cause.

Shortness of breath and a dry cough lasting longer than they would if they were just from a bad cold.

Marks on the Skin, pink or purple blotches which appear all over the body and look like bruises or blisters.

But remember, each of these symptoms is quite common and may be due to some other cause. It is only when they all occur together—and last for a long time—that there may be reason for concern. Even then, only laboratory tests can prove whether someone has AIDS.

Treatment—There is no treatment for AIDS. All of those diagnosed as having had AIDS for more than two years, have died. AIDS has now appeared in thirty three countries and all inhabited continents. In India, first case of AIDS was reported in 1986.

Condoms and vaginal foam are partial barrier to all diseases. Check that your intended partner has no obvious signs of infection. If your suspicion persists, postpone genital contact. This may nip a new relationship in the bud but you won't end up with gonorrhoea, herp, AIDS etc. Be careful with any new partner especially if you know he or she has had a lot of anonymous relationships.

The risk of disease is accepted as the price of sexual freedom. If you promiscuously ride the sexual merry-go-round, the odds are against you.

❑❑

Birth Control Techniques

In recent times, more and more families in the world have voluntarily and successfully imposed a limit on the number of children they have inspite of strong opposition from various religious groups. Birth control is the most crying need of our time, at least for India. Our population has already crossed the 100 crore mark.

Many people, even well educated are uninformed about conception. They do not realise that pregnancy can occur from a single act of intercourse or that the few drops of fluid that sometimes appear on the tip of the penis during the excitement contain sperm which can be tranferred by hand or penis to the vagina. Whenever a woman is ovulating there is the possibility of conception. And contrary to popular belief, ovulation can occur even during menstruation period.

Reproduction can be prevented at any stage of the reproductive process, before or after conception or after birth. The birth control methods fall into two categories: Reversible methods and Irreversible methods.

THE REVERSIBLE METHODS OF BIRTH CONTROL

The Pill

The pill is a birth control drug containing synthetic oestrogen and progesterone in dosages that alter normal menstruation so that ovulation does not occur. When it first came out, the number of side effects reported made many women reluctant to use it. But modern research has reduced many of these by discovering that a milder dosage is just as effective and is safer for use over a long period of time. The modern pill is the result of dogged research and concerted efforts of many researchers. They realised that during pregnancy, when ovulation and periods cease, levels of oestrogens and progesterone in the blood are naturally high. If they could manage to produce a state of pseudopregnancy by giving extra doses of these hormones, ovulation would be halted and conception would not occur. There are more than hundred different contraceptive pills in use worldwide.

The pill is 99% reliable provided it is taken regularly for a fixed number of days within a 28-day cycle. It is not expensive either.

Some women feel side effects such as nausea or changes in menstrual flow. The pill is not recommended to any woman after the age of forty. There is no evidence that the pill encourages breast cancer, on the contrary it may actually reduce such risks.

Withdrawal and other Methods

Withdrawal method is also considered as contraceptive method in which the male withdraws the penis from the vagina just before ejaculation. But this technique is not reliable because the penis often releases semen containing sperm even before ejaculation, and because many men find it difficult to withdraw near the peak of sexual excitement.

The only advantage of withdrawal is that it is better than nothing. Other behavioural methods, such as oral sex is much more effective, though they too cause frustration and are not to everyone's liking.

In most women, breast feeding postpones ovulation and therefore, chances of conception for about six months after child birth are very less.

Douching is also regarded as useless contraceptive procedure, by the time it happens, many sperms have already entered the uterus and begun their journey towards the oviduct.

Rhythm Method

Couples using the rhythm method avoid sexual intercourse when they think the woman is at her most fertile. But this is not a very reliable method because it is difficult for the woman to know exactly when she is ovulating and there is no really safe time when a woman can be sure she will not get pregnant.

The two more reliable rhythm methods require that she checks, daily and without fail, either her body temperature on waking or the nature and amount of mucus around her cervix. Both these methods are highly unnatural practices for most women. It requires not only a regular and predictable life style but also a strong degree of motivation and discipline. The temperature methods cannot be relied upon until the woman has recorded her temperature daily for a minimum of six months. She then has to determine when, within each cycle, there is consistent rise in temperature following after a consistent low.

Three days after the rise has peaked, coitus is allowable until the onset of next period.

The cervical mucus method monitors daily discharge from the cervix. A day or two before the ovulation, mucus taken from the cervix turns from cloudy and sticky to clear and stringy in consistency.

The safe period starts four days after the clear mucus appears and lasts until the onset of the next period, after which the mucus changes back to cloudy.

Another method of determining a safe period is to monitor the menstrual cycle for six or twelve months and then, assuming that subsequent cycles will be similar. It helps in recognising the danger zone, usually ten to nineteen days before the start of the next period. The remainder of the cycle is safe.

Unfortunately predictability is poor since most women have highly irregular menstrual cycles.

Condoms

A condom is a thin rubber sheath which unrolls to fit over a man's erect penis. It can be used during sexual intercourse between a man and woman to help prevent the woman from becoming pregnant and lower the risk of sexually transmitted infection. It is also useful in premature ejaculation because it usually slows up the orgasm. A condom must be put on before the penis touches the vaginal area. A condom can only be used once. After it has been used, it should be wrapped in a tissue and put in a dustbin. They are available free from Family Planning Centres. It is the most widely used contraceptive device throughout the world.

Cervical Caps and Diaphragms

A diaphragm is a method of contraception for women. It is also called a cap or Dutch cap. It is a thin rubber dome with a bendy rim. It covers the cervix and works as a barrier stopping sperm from getting into the uterus and fertilizing an ovum. The woman puts the diaphragm in her vagina before having sexual intercourse. When it is in the right place, neither the man nor the woman can feel it. To prevent pregnancy, it is smeared with spermicide before putting it in. After intercourse it should remain there at least for six hours. She can then take it out, dry it and put it away until she needs to use it again. A physician or a trained nurse can help you to find the diaphragm of correct size and can fit it properly. It can be inserted some hours before coitus. It should not be left in place for more than 24 hours, neither it should be removed atleast six hours after coitus. It does not suit all women.

Creams, Foams, Jellies and Suppositories

These are chemical contraceptives that either kill sperm or make conditions inside the vagina hostile to their passage. Inserted with a finger or using a simple applicator, they are the only female birth control methods that do not require medical supervision. Many couples complain they interfere with sexual pleasure because they have to be inserted shortly before intercourse, and most of them taste bad, which makes oral sex unpleasant. They also provide extra lubrication and a degree of protection against certain type of veneral diseases.

Intra-Uterine Devices (IUD)

These are plastic or metal devices which are placed in the uterus and stay there for a few years. They come in many shapes—Rings, bows, Ts, Xs, and would probably work even if they looked like a mini spoon or toy battleship. The elongated S-shaped Lippes Loop is the standard device. Each shape has its pros and cons. Attempts to make the perfect IUD have now produced active IUDs with added copper or hormones.

An IUD reduces the likelihood of the zygote implanting itself in the uterus wall and make the intrauterine environment more hostile to sperm because foreign objects in the uterus prevent conception. It is easy to insert into the uterus, is cheap, does not interfere with body chemistry and can be left in place for long periods and forgotten about except for the occasional check. It is also easy to remove if pregnancy is desired.

For some women it is not suitable because it causes heavier than usual menstrual bleeding, occasional cramps and in a few cases interferes with sexual activity. There is also an increased risk of infection of the uterus or fallopian tubes.

THE IRREVERSIBLE METHODS OF BIRTH
Control Sterilisation

Rendering an individual incapable of reproduction is called sterilisation. It is a permanent method of contraception for both men and women. Male sterilisation is called **Vasectomy**. The female sterilisation is called **Tubectomy**.

Vasectomy

Vasectomy involves making two small cuts in the scrotum in order to snip the duct known as **Vas Deferens** on each side and tie off the cut ends, so that sperm cannot travel into the man's urethra and out of his penis. After a man has been sterilised, and once his semen no longer contains sperm, he cannot make a woman pregnant. But he can still have erection, ejaculate and enjoy sex in the same way that he did before he was sterilised. A trained doctor can do this operation in ten to twenty minutes. After that, men are advised to take it easy and refrain from intercourse for several days but otherwise they can go back to work or continue with their usual routine within hours.

Since live sperms remain in the Vasa and urethra for some time after vasectomy contraception must continue to be used for atleast fifteen or so ejaculations or until the ejaculation is free of sperm. This operation is done under a local anaesthetic so there is no pain.

Tubectomy

Female sterilisation involves closing off both **Fallopian Tubes** so that **Ova** cannot travel into the uterus. This means that the woman cannot get pregnant. But she still has menstrual periods and can enjoy sex in the same way that she did before she was sterilised. She still ovulates normally, but the egg is absorbed by the body instead of being shed during the period. This operation is also very simple now.

Very occasionally, the sterilisation operation is not a success because the vas deferens or fallopian tubes rejoin.

Sterilisation should be regarded as a once and for all procedure. It is not reversible. Though it is safer procedure for men than women, yet more women are sterilised than men because it is the women that bear the brunt of pregnancy. Feelings of inadequacy or depression after sterilisation are not unusual. After all, fertility is a strong symbol of femininity and masculinity.

Researchers are now developing sterilisation techniques that do not involve surgery. Our government is encouraging such operations and offering a number of incentives as a part of birth control measures.

There is now such a wide array of family planning methods that most couples and individuals should be able to find at least one that meet their needs.

❑❑

Sexual Potency

The ability of the male to achieve and maintain an erection, and to ejaculate to perform sexual intercourse is called sexual potency.

Even within normal limits, male sexual potency varies considerably from man to man. It depends on age, constitution, temperament, race, habits, practice, erotic influences, psychic influences and interests other than erotic in character, and many other circumstances.

There are both sexually weak men as well as sexual athletes. This special aptitude or deficiency has nothing to do with general physical weakness or vigour.

It is determined by the special glands secreting the sperm, or it may depend to some degree on the amount of fluid expelled on each occasion by the **Prostate Gland and Seminal Vesicles.**

Some men declare they can voluntarily retain or hold back a portion of their ejaculate, if they wish to follow the first coitus by a second, soon after. There is no exact knowledge of the causes. But there are perfectly healthy and normal men in their most vigorous years who can only execute coitus twice a week, and at the most in exceptional circumstances, once a day. There are others who can repeat the act three or four or more times in succession, or at very brief intervals during several days without any injury to their health and zest.

Sexual Incapacity

When more is demanded sexually from any man than he can perform, his body simply refuses. In spite of the most acute excitations, his discharge does not occur. This temporary and occasional apathy is quite normal, it is in contrast to the genuine impotence, which fails before quite moderate incitement and is distinctly morbid.

The occasional sexual incapacity of the healthy man is not only normal but beneficial. It is a natural self-defence of the organism against exactions and excesses.

If more is habitually expected, it damages a man's general health. If further ejaculations are expected after the available supply has been spent, great efforts are needed from the brain and body to produce the state of tension necessary for the effective collaboration in the genital act.

Excessive sexual activity may cause slight pains across the loins, and more important diminished clarity and concentration in brain work. This harmful effect should be avoided, as it may quickly become obstinate, and possibly chronic.

Successive Acts

Two or even three successive acts of coitus can be of great advantage after a few or longer period of abstinence. After abstinence when intercourse is performed the man often ejaculates very soon not just enough to gratify the woman. In such cases coitus will give both partners relief. Nothing is more fatal to love than disappointment in sexual intercourse.

The first relative failure may be redeemed by a prompt repetition of communion. It should occur immediately or after an hour or so. It depends on man's own potency, mutual inclination and on so many other factors.

Don't recklessly habituate your wife to a degree of sexual frequency and intensity, which you may be quite unable to keep up, for any length of time. When once she is introduced to the maximum of sexual pleasure. You won't be able to modify her desires when this maximum will no longer be available. It may destroy marital peace and happiness. It may cause chronic sexual over strain and fatigue on your own. This may reduce you to a mental and physical weakling, a neurotic.

☐☐

Impotence

Impotence is a male sexual dysfunction characterised by inability to achieve or maintain an erection sufficient for performance of sexual intercourse. It may also take the form of coitus without ejaculation, orgasm without pleasure, and lack of interest in sex.

The problem of impotence has become quite common. An estimated 10% of men are incapable of getting a firm penis no matter how physically or psychologically stimulated they become. As many as 50% of men experience impotence some of the time. In fact nearly all men struggle with impotence at least once in their lives.

When the first time a man suffers from impotence, he may become anxious and begin to question his manhood. The second time, his anxiety builds and what happened previously takes on greater emotional significance. The third bout of impotence may actually be brought on by recalling the prior incidents.

Repetition sets up a vicious cycle of Psychogenic caused by the mind's impotence, which adds to any actual physical problem. Obviously treatment of impotence must begin with finding the cause.

If a man has sexual desires but fails to get or hold an erection when excited—with partner and from masturbation—and does not have erection during sleep or upon awakening, his problem has an organic or physical basis.

Functional Impotence

It is caused due to failure to achieve or maintain a penile erection because of circulatory or nervous system disorders, effects of aging, anxiety, stress or excessive use of Alcohol or Drugs including many medications taken for high blood pressure.

New Impotence

Impotence in young men that has been attributed due to a feeling of sexual insecurity as a result of women's liberation. The liberated women are sexually more demanding. This demand is threatening some men and causing impotence in them.

Organic Impotence

It is the inability to achieve and maintain an erection because of any physical defects in the genitalia or the nervous system tract that controls erection.

Primary Impotence

It is extreme sexual impotence in which a man has never been able to achieve erection sufficient for intercourse.

Psychic Impotence

It is functional incapacity of the male to perform satisfactory sexual intercourse inspite of desire and intact genital organs. The condition may take the form of premature or retarded ejaculation, or of inability to achieve or maintain erection and expel seminal fluid. Psychologists trace this disorder to such factors as refusing to give up castration fears, unresolved attachments to the mother and association of sex with dirt and filth.

Secondary Impotence

It is a condition in which a male has been able to achieve a normal erection and ejaculation in intercourse, but is not able to repeat the performance. This type of impotence is very common.

Treatment of Impotence

Impotence is treated through a therapeutic process in which the primary objective is that of overcoming the **fear of failure** factor in impotence. The therapy requires the active participation of the sexual partner and the creation of an atmosphere in which the male does not feel any pressure to perform, but instead is allowed to relax and enjoy contact, pleasures and the emotional interaction of love making. The process may involve stimulating the penis to an erection several times without requiring coitus.

Special exercises are given for this purpose under the Masters and Johnson treatment programme.

Chelation Therapy

One solution for impotent men could be chelation therapy. It is a safe and effective way to open clogged arteries and increase blood flow to the area of the body with impaired blood circulation. The chief agent used to clear arteries is a synthetic amino called **Ethylene Diamine Tetracetic Acid (EDTA)**. For this purpose intravenous injections are administered.

Inability to Sustain Erection

The erection process is a physical phenomenon that begins with an increased flow of blood into the penis and ends with the blood slowly returning to the body's general circulation.

Sometimes the blood starts to recede sluggishly while the erection is still in progress because of a contraction of blood vessel valves in the penis. This decreases the hardness of the erection.

A number of medical scientists believe that the erection valves become rigid as part of the aging process and lose the ability to contract or relax. Hardening of the arteries, which often accompanies aging may narrow the erection the penis and producing the degree of hardness a man experienced when he was young.

Thus the main causes of impotence in middle aged men are clogging of blood circulation in the penis, dropping of penile blood pressure, lack of mobility of penile vein valves, and a combination of all these factors.

Many prescription drugs also affect sexual performance, causing impotence, delayed ejaculation, retrograde ejaculation, loss of libido, or even development of female sex characteristics in men.

❏❏

Infertility

The inability to have children is called infertility. This condition affects one in ten or twelve couples. In 60% of cases female partner is responsible and in 40% of cases male partner is responsible.

Causes of Infertility

Common physical causes in the male are low sperm count, failure to deposit sperm in the vagina and obstruction of the *epididymis, vas deferens* or *ejaculatory duct*.

Causes in the female are failure to produce a sufficient number of healthy eggs, partial or complete obstruction of the fallopian tubes, endometriosis, rejection of the fertilized egg, and pelvic tumours.

There may also be any psychological cause like excessive tension, in either the male or female.

Almost all the newly weds plan to have children. The reason may be psychological or biological. Self worth is often seen in terms of children. People want children to satisfy family and society at large, to achieve personal growth and fulfilment.

It is also required to conform to religious, political or cultural teachings. Children are also a means of rationalizing sexual activities, a demonstration of sexual potency, an affirmation of masculinity or feminity.

There are even reports that in some men the regular wearing of tight underpants or taking long hot baths is associated with infertility. These raise the temperature of the scrotum.

Infertile couples now have two main options if they cannot or do not wish to adopt children or if fertility drugs are not the solution. These are—Artificial Insemination (AI) and In-Vitro Fertilization (IVF).

Artificial Insemination

Artificial insemination involves collecting sperm from the husband or from a donor and introducing it into the uterus at a time when the chances of conceiving are greater. The sperm sample is usually obtained by masturbation. It may be fresh, or it may have been frozen for several months.

If the husband has low sperm count or physically incapable of coitus. It may be necessary for him to make several donations, or his donations may be supplemented by those of a donor. If his sperms are defective, the sample used for insemination will come from a donor alone.

In-Vitro Fertilisation

This alternative procedure, is used when the woman's oviducts are irrevocably blocked. An egg is removed from or near the ovary. Then it is mixed with sperm. After a period of development in a glass laboratory dish, it is introduced into the uterus to await implantation. This process is also known as Test Tube Baby. In a number of countries, this technique has proved successful. Attempts to make IVF more widely suitable and available are continuing. The chances of success are 50:50. But various religious institutions have condemned it as immoral. Moreover the cost of this method is very high.

Surrogate Parenting

A woman who takes the place of a sterile wife for the purpose of insemination by the husband is called **Surrogate Mother**. But surrogate motherhood is the subject of legal dispute as to the rights of the surrogate mother over the child she bears.

But this practice of one woman bearing a baby on behalf of another, is now becoming more common. A number of women are willingly coming forward to offer themselves for hire to conceive and bear children for others.

But with these New Age benefits, a terrific hue and cry is also being raised by the religious leaders. They oppose commercialisation of child bearing for others. Even then the emotional investment of the surrogate mother, who surrenders the baby she has been carrying for nine months is easier to imagine. Some women treat it as a business deal. This process is very very costly.

A few women feel that it would be wonderful to keep having babies without the responsibility of raising them. Many men and women are willing to offer surrogate services free of charge.

Infertility Clinic

An Infertility clinic is that place where men and women, who are finding it difficult to start a baby, can go for help and guidance.

❏❏

Aphrodisiacs and Anaphrodisiacs

Food, drinks and drugs which stimulate sexual desire and activity are called aphrodisiac. But there is no scientific proof that any substance can do this.

Aphrodisiacs

People have been seeking the ultimate aphrodisiac for as long as they have been searching for the formula, to change iron into gold. For thousands of years, people in every part of the world have tried different items, internal and external, to enhance sexual response.

The psychological basis for some aphrodisiacal claim is that when the substance is eaten, drunk or rubbed on the body, it acts on nerve centres in the brain to decrease inhibitions.

Substances considered aphrodisiacs have varied from human breast milk to the powder derived from ground up dried beetles, to cherry pits, which contain stimulants.

These many eatables numbering about 2,000 have been applied as potency aids, sexual stimulators, or the means for getting in the mood.

Modern Western societies have been making aphrodisiacs in laboratories. These artificial substances have included drugs such as **Estrogens** and **Androgens**. The modern aphrodisiacs have replaced the Elixir, Herbs and Amulets of the ancient times.

In reality, till date there is no single love potion for raising the libido.

Effects of Foods and Drinks on Desire and Potency

There are a number of solid and liquid varieties of nourishment calculated to incite sexual desire, intensify sexual pleasure and favour potency or efficiency in the sexual act. A number of sex-manuals describe not only the various dishes which promote sexual stimulation, but their preparation and ingredients. But many of these recipes are obviously fantastic, and recognisable as such at a glance.

Every society believe in some special foods and preparations which have erotic effects and increase potency. There are abundant of foods that excite sexual activitiy and underfeeding inhibits these functions.

It is generally believed that meat is stimulating. Eggs have a reputation for tonic efficacy, both as a stimulant and a restorative after special exertions in coitus. It is believed that an egg diet favours the production of spermatozoa. Fish is also regarded as stimulating.

Vegetarians believe that milk-rice dishes, beetroots, carrots, dates and turnip are said to resemble eggs in quality.

At one time potatoes and tomatoes were looked on as "Love Foods". Eating them conferred sexual and reproductive bliss. As long as they were exotic and difficult to obtain they kept their mystique. But once in common use, their love enhancing power was discredited. The rarity of truffles today allows them to keep their reputation as aphrodisiacs.

Condiments like saffron, cinnamon, vanila,

pepper, peppermint, ginger, fennel, etc. are regarded as stimulating.

The Ancient Hindus mixed fennel juice with milk, honey, sugar and licorice for an aphrodisiac.

Chocolate is also regarded as aphrodisiac.

A European herb licorice with purple flower, spices and a root that contain a sweet substance used in confectionary and medicines is also used as an aphrodisiac. It is taken along with vallerian, clove and nutmeg.

Thyme, a small grey green shrub, that has been the source of medicines and food flavourings is believed to have aphrodisiac quality.

Celery, artichokes, asparagus are used in the Western countries for stimulation purpose.

Honey, dates and milk are also believed to have stimulating qualities. Dry-fruits like almonds, cashewnuts, currant, pistachio are also in the list. Spanishfly, mandrake and yohimibine are also used by people in the west.

Spanishfly

Spanishfly is the common name for a powder made from ground **Cantharis Beetles**, the powder is a powerful irritant which can inflame the skin as well as the lining of the digestive and excretory track. Though it can cause erection, yet there is a price to pay. The erection is usually painful, not pleasurable - a reflex reaction due to pelvic irritation.

Women given spanishfly may begin to moan, but this is a moan of pain, not arousal. It may cause ulceration in the digestive and urinary tract. Therefore spanishfly is not only ineffective as a love potion but also highly dangerous. It is popular in European countries and USA.

Mandrake Roots

Mandrake roots are reputed to be efficacious because of their resemblance to the penis. It is native herb of Northern Africa and Southern Europe. For centuries, it has been used as a narcotic, analgesic, hallucinogen and alleged aphrodisiac.

The active principle in mandrake roots are Atropine and Scopolamine, both of which are sleep-inducing. Mandrake causes mental confusion and hampers respiration.

Yohimibine

Yohimibine is an alkaloid obtained from the bark of yohimbe tree which grows in West Central Africa. It is used as an alleged male aphrodisiac.

Shilajeet

Shilajeet is popular in India as an Ayurvedic aphrodisiac. It is a kind of bitumen which is used with milk.

Sympathetic Medicines

Many folk preparations from around the world come under the heading **Sympathetic Medicines**. Their efficacy comes from their similarity to the body organ or process in question. The horn of Rhinoceros or deer represents a firm, erect penis. Olives represent testes and oysters as vaginal labia. Pepper creates a sensation of heat and cooked okra represent vaginal lubrication.

Belief in such sympathetic potential is a feature of various homeopathic therapies and magical procedures. The success of such remedies is usually quite coincidental, or the result of the extra care and sensitivity that accompany the situation in which they are given or taken. If they do not work, it can always be said that they were not prepared or used properly.

When the partners conspire to use a love potion, the result is often self-fulfilling prophecy.

Organs from Animals

Testes or testes extracts are quite commonly used as male aphrodisiacs and rejuvenators. Sheep testes are enjoyed as gourmet delicacies but are without special powers. Injectables from these and other animal tissues are considered unethical in a few countries.

Every culture has its own special aphrodisiacs. To this day many rhinos, elephants, deer, sheep and other animals lose their lives so that their penises, testes, horns, tusks or other organs can be used to improve the sex lives of those who believe in their efficacy. Technologically advanced societies put their faith in other kinds of aphrodisiacs.

Cola and asprin, for example, were considered a good bet about sixty years ago and more lately marijuana or cannabis.

Pharmaceuticals

Cocaine is increasingly used, although illegally as a recreational drug and has some reputation as an aphrodisiac. When it is inhaled like a snuff or taken intravenously; the resulting **High** often gives a feeling of power and with a feeling of potency and desirability.

Erections are often prolonged and orgasm delayed, for those who think longer is better, this is viewed as a plus, as in the drug-induced sense of accomplishment.

Sexual drawbacks also exist. Extended cocaine use can lead to Priapism, a prolonged painful erection in men and prolonged vaginal dryness in women. In both senses cocaine use can lead to an extension of copulation time but an inability to reach orgasm.

Other drugs reputed to enhance sexual experience are **Amyl Nitrite** and **Isobutyl Nitrite**. These drugs induce physiological changes—increased heart rate and blood flow. It may be personally interpreted as signs of sexual excitement. These drugs sold as volatile liquids, are usually inhaled at the start of sex play, or at impending orgasm. They are not necessarily innocuous. Increased blood flow can have detrimental effect if one happens to suffer from heart, cerebrovascular or eye disease.

Viagra is also very widely used in many countries. It is very popular to increase stimulation.

Easily available drugs such as Amphetamines, Antidepressants, Tranquilizers, Stimulants and Antipsychotic preparations account for more than 60% of all prescriptions. When depression and anxiety are relieved, Libido and Potency tend to increase. In many people Amphetamines and Stimulants seem to energise sexual response. But the effects vary from person to person.

Among tonics are some such, as the various combinations of Phosphorus, which have a decidedly strong positive influence, sexually. Others again diminish general tension and inhibit, the function of bladder and bowels but stimulate desire; the chief of these is Opium with its derivatives.

In Ayurvedic medical system oxides of gold and silver have also aphrodisiac effects. Gold and silver leaves are also used.

Placebo Medicines
Alcohol

It is said that "drink provokes the desire, but it takes away the performance." Perhaps the most widely used sexual stimulant is alcohol.

In small amount its invigorating influence is universally admitted. But in large quantities, it paralyses the genital function on the physical side, while at the same time it breaks down psychic inhibitions and controls. Habitual drunkenness is extremely harmful to the sexual organs and functions. In men, impotence due to alcohol is common.

Tea, Coffee, Tobacco

Excessive use of tea, coffee and tobacco also produce unfavourable results like alcohol.

Acid drinks such as lemonade, in large quantities, seem generally to diminish sexual desire.

Marijuana

Prolonged marijuana use severely reduces both sexual activity and sperm production in man because it depresses the production of androgen. But like alcohol it certainly reduces inhibitions.

Marijuana appears to be effective because the persons using them expect a specific result and act in such a way that their expectations become reality. This is the Famous Placebo Effect at Work. The situations in which such drugs are used often reflect a tacit understanding that sexual activity will follow.

Harmless Devices

There are a few aids which have no harmful reaction. These are hot cushions, or pillows applied at the lumber region, sitz baths or hip baths, massage and special exercises.

Anaphrodisiacs

Anaphrodisiacs are those substances that reliably decrease arousal or enthusiasm for sex. These are used in the treatment of various sex offenders. Although their list is very long, yet the list of drugs producing the desired result is short.

Salt petre known as Potassium Nitrate is the most

often mentioned anaphrodisiacs. But in large doses it can be fatal. It can increase the urine flow.

Heroin, opium and other opiates are effective anaphrodisiacs, with their sedative and anaesthetic effects. These drugs diminish libido, potency and orgasm. Sexual interest is replaced by passivity and a craving for the drug itself. These are banned in most countries.

Barbiturates are indeed downers when it comes to sex. Like alcohol, they take away inhibition. But with increased use they also take away sexual interest and potency. In women who abuse barbiturates menstrual and ovulatory abnormalities are common.

Pharmaceutical companies have been successful in developing several anti-sexual drugs. One is Cyproterone Accetate (CA) which acts by competing with testosterone so that the hormone can not do its work. The drug reduces the libido, erectile potential and orgasmic capacity.

A Warning

A layman should not touch these powerful toxic substances, either in concentrated form, or masked among much advertised Secret Remedies to restore virility, without professional consultation and advice.

Impotence is a serious and complex condition. It may arise from so many different causes that its treatment is a matter for medical specialist. Attempts to force up sexual desires and the normal degree of sexual vigour, by powerful artificial means, must sooner or later cause damage.

Don't jump into the nets of the Quacks. The quacks and fake physicians earn their gold by feeding the gullible with lots of so-called high potency giving medicines which do show favourable effects initially, but the users have to suffer so seriously later that they really become sexually impotent because of the harmful effects of those medicines.

◻◻

Old-Age Sexual Problems

According to the findings of Kinsey and his associates only about one fourth of all males become impotent by the age of 70. Even here many cases are due to psychological factors only.

More recent studies have indicated that men and women in their 80's and 90's are quite capable of enjoying sex.

Sexual Response

Every mental and physical aspect of each phase of the sexual response cycle changes with age. The changes are slow and subtle, and vary according to the constitution, health and the mental outlook of the person concerned. But with a receptive and active sexual partner the changes will be slower. But if sexual opportunities are infrequent they may be quicker.

New Outlook on Old-Age Sex

Until recently it was believed that women past the menopause and men over 50 lost interest in sex. This reflected the convention that tied sex to child bearing capacity. Sex in later life was subject for ridicule carrying the image of **Dirty Old Man** and the **Frustrated Old Woman**. This idea of the senior citizens indulging in sex damaged the dignity that the elderly are supposed to have. The young are often reluctant to see their parents or grand parents as sexual beings.

Research findings indicate that the assumption

that old age is non-sexual or neuter was found to be a myth.

Many researchers reported that while ageing was accompanied by a general decline in frequency of sexual activities, but much depended on previous experience, parent attitude and aspiration for the future.

It has also been observed that in general, Those who arrive early at the party stay late, and those who came late leave early.

Changes in Old Age

In men as the age advances, erection is slower, coitus less urgent and orgasm delayed. Each phase and mechanism in the sexual response changes at its own rate. At first the intensity of orgasm is to weaken and if one lives long enough, it will fade completely. Then erectile ability declines.

Women have to contend with more physical changes as they age than men. This is largely due to the rapid decrease in female hormones, at the menopause between the age of 45 and 55. The discomfort of dryness in the vagina is also felt.

Parents who face ageing realistically and adjust accordingly find no diminished pleasure in sex.

Organ Atrophy

The wasting and shrinking of an organ or tissue such as the testicles is known as organ atrophy.

If any organ is not used at all or used a very little it starts to develop atrophies. Inactivity of the testicles help to bring about premature senility and degeneracy. It makes the people sad and without enthusiasm. It also causes physical weakness.

On the other hand moderate and suitable use of the sexual function—which is possible up to a very great age—keeps the whole organism comparatively vigorous and efficient.

That is why doctors often advise the ageing people to continue regular sexual intercourse, in the fifties and sixties, unless specific morbid symptoms counter indicate.

❑❑

Psychosexual Disorders

Psychosexual disorders are a group of sexual disorders stemming from psychological rather than organic factors, and comprising gender identity disorders, paraphillias, psychosexual dysfunctions, ego-dystonic homosexuality and nymphomania etc.

Paraphilia

Paraphilia is distorted form of sexuality in which sexual excitement is achieved in unusual ways. They include coprophilia, exhibitionism, fetishism, frotteurism, klismaphilia, misophilia, neurophilia, paedophilia, sexual masochism, sexual sadism, telephone scatalogia, transvestism, voyeurism, and zoophilia.

Homosexuality

Sexual preference for members of one's own sex, based on mutual attraction that may be limited to sexual fantasies and feelings, is called **Homosexuality**. It usually involves overt sexual activities ranging from kissing, fondling, friction and mutual masturbation to fellatio and intercourse. Anilingus among men and cunnilingus and tribadism among women.

Tribadism is a lesbian practice in which one partner lies on top of the other and stimulates coitus by rubbing the genitals together.

Female homosexuals are called **Lesbian,** male homosexuals are called **Gay** and hetrosexuals are called **straight**.

Psychosexual Disorders

Alternate Sexual Life Style

In our society hetrosexuality has been regarded as the appropriate mode of sexual behaviour, while homosexuality has been regarded as a mental dis-order and homosexuals as **Sick Persons** in need of treatment.

On the basis of various research findings, homosexuality is now regarded as an alternate sexual life style. In a number of countries homosexuality is now legal. The majority of homosexuals accept their homosexuality, fulfill their responsible social roles. They have no more personality maladjustment than do hetrosexuals. Homosexual individuals are marrying each other and living together.

In a number of countries they have separate bars, theaters and other business establishments which may cater primarily to homosexual individuals.

Female homosexuals may also exchange rings and marital vows in formal ceremonies. Lesbians place greater emphasis on the quality of their interpersonal relationship and less on its sexual aspects.

Causes of Homosexuality

Some investigators view biological factors as playing the key role in the development of homosexual behaviour.

1. *Genetic and Hormonal Factors*

   According to a number of investigators homosexuality results from an abnormal **Androgen-Estrogen** ratio.

2. *Homosexual Experiences and their Positive Reinforcement*

   It is also associated with pleasant homosexual experiences during adolescence or early adulthood.

3. *Negative Conditioning of Heterosexual Behaviour*

When any boy or girl is ridiculed, rebuked, rebuffed and humiliated in his effort to approach members of the opposite sex he or she may turn towards homosexuality as source of affection and sexual outlet. Early sexual relations under unfortunate circumstances may have a comparable effect.

4. *Family Patterns*

Family patterns may create a wide range of adjustment problems and even severe maladjustment. A dominant seductive mother and a weak or absent father or a mother frustrated by an unhappy marital relationship may establish homosexual relations.

5. *General Socio-cultural Factors*

The severity of social sanctions for deviations may markedly influence the incidence of homosexual and other unconventional sexual life styles.

Various surveys show that perhaps one in two adults is likely to have had one or more experiences involving someone of the same sex, and that at least half of those who haven't have felt sexually attracted to someone of their own sex.

When people are confined to single-sex institutions like prisons, boarding schools, ships on long voyages, for extended period of time, their sexual preferences tend to bend somewhat towards what is available.

In societies where homosexuality is accepted, it will be open and public, but where it is regarded as perversion, it will be forced underground.

The fact is that there has been no society, and no time in history, when homosexuality has not existed. It occurs among very primitive peoples and in advanced societies. In ancient Greece and Rome, for example male homosexuality was open, accepted and common, and held to be very pure and high form of life.

It is now recognised that people who prefer same-sex are not **sick** physically or mentally. They are perfectly happy to be the way they are. That is the reason why they are called **Gay**.

Homosexuality is still stuck with some of the old labels—"Not natural", "Against nature". Though these are slowly fading. The taboos against homosexuality are really the old thinking of sex is only for reproduction. Discovering that someone is a homosexual, comes as a shock to most people.

Incest

Culturally prohibited sexual relations between family members such as a father and daughter, brother and sister, mother and son etc. are called Incest.

In every society incestuous behaviour does occur. But its actual incidence is unknown since it takes place in a family setting and are the least reported.

Social taboos or law against incest are found in particularly all societies but the degree of relationship may differ from society to society.

These are the Main Causes of Incest

1. *Accidental Incest*

   It may happen when brothers and sisters share the same bedroom during preadolescent or adolescent period. They may tend to engage in sexual exploration and experimentation.

2. *Severe Psychopathology*

Individuals such as alcoholics and psychotics may indulge themselves in incestuous relation with the lowering of their inner control.

3. *Paedophilia*

It may happen when a father has an intense craving for young children as sex objects including his own daughter.

4. *A faulty Pattern Model*

When a father sets an undesirable example for his son by engaging in incestous relations with his daughter, and may encourage his son to do like wise.

5. *Family Pathology and Disturbed Marital Relations*

When any family has low morals or is disorganised, a rejecting hostile wife may encourage such relations.

Paedophilia

Paedophilia is a psychosexual disorder in which an adult desires sexual relations with a child. The sexual activity may consist of heterosexual intercourse, fellatio, or anal intercourse. It may also be limited to looking and touching occasionally. The child is induced to manipulate the sex organs of the paedophiliac or to engage in mouth-genital contacts. In most cases the victim is known to the offender and usually there is no physical coercion.

The main causes of Paedophilia are :

1. *Immature Personality*

The person who has never been able to establish or maintain satisfactory interpersonal sexual relationship. He feels sexually comfortable only with children.

2. *The Regressed Offenders*

It may happen when any person discovers that his wife or girlfriend is having an affair with another man.

3. *The Conditioned Offenders*
   Those individuals who have had their definite sexual experiences with young boys. This conditioned behaviour continues into adulthood in terms of sexual preference.

4. *The Psychopathic Offenders*
   Those who prey on children in search of new sexual thrills. Such offenders usually have a history of antisocial behaviour.

Sodomy

Sexual intercourse between a man and another man is called sodomy. The sodomy is derived from the ancient city of Sodom where corruption was so rampant that it was destroyed. Sodomy is regarded as unnatural sexual intercourse.

Avisodomy

Avisodomy is the sexual intercourse between a human male and a bird. The birds commonly used for this purpose are—chickens, ducks, geese and turkey because of their accomodating anatomy. This practise seems to be worldwide, as old as human history, and still quite current.

Bestiality

Sexual relations with animals through intercourse, masturbation, fellatio, rubbing, anal penetration or having one's genital licked is called bestiality. It also includes deriving sexual pleasure and excitement from observing the sexual activities of animals and from a fetish based upon animal furs or skin.

Zoophilia

Zoophilia is a psychosexual disorder in which farm animals or household pets are persistently preferred or exclusively used to achieve sexual excitement.

Sadism

Sadism is a psychosexual disorder, or paraphilia in which sexual excitement is obtained by inflicting pain on the sexual partner. Sadist act may consist of physical cruelty, such as flogging or bondage, or mental cruelty as in humiliating the partner. The suffering may be inflicted on either a consenting or a non-consenting person, and may range from mild injury to raping, torturing or even killing the victim. Full sexual gratification is obtained from the sadist practice. A sadist may even slash a woman with a razor or prick her with a needle, experiencing an orgasm in the process.

These are the main causes for Sadism:

1. *Negative Attitude Towards Sex*

   Sadist activities may protect an individual with negative attitudes toward sex from the full sexual implications of his behaviour, and at the same time may help him express his contempt and punishment of the other person for engaging in sexual relation. For many sexually inadequate and insecure individuals, the infliction of pain is apparently a safe means of achieving sexual stimulation, strong feelings of power and superiority over his victim may for the time being shut out underlying feelings of inadequacy and anxiety.

2. *Painful Experience*

   It may also be due to any experience in which sexual excitation and possibly orgasm have been associated with the infliction of pain.

Psychosexual Disorders / 103

3. **Psychopathological Condition**

   It may also happen due to lowering of inner controls and the deviations of symbolic processes as in Schizophrenia and other severe form of psychopathology.

Masochism

It is a psychological disorder in which the individual persistently derives pleasure from pain inflicted on the self instead of on others as in the case of sadism.

Masochistic behaviour usually comes about through conditioned learning, as a result of early experiences. An individual comes to associate pain with sexual pleasure.

Voyeurism

In this disorder an individual derives sexual satisfaction from secretly observing people in the nude or in the act of undressing or engaging in sexual activity. Scotophilia and inspectionalism are also synonymous terms.

Viewing the body of an attractive female seems to be quite stimulating sexually for many males. The privacy and mystery that have traditionally surrounded sexual activities has tended to increase curiosity about them. If a youth with such curiosity feels shy and inadequate in his relations with the other sex, it is not surprising for him to accept the substitute of peeping. In this way he satisfies his curiosity and to some extent meets his sexual needs without the trauma of actually approaching a female. Peeping activities often provide important compensatory feelings of power and superiority on the one being looked at.

Exhibitionism

Exhibitionism is a psychosexual disorder, or paraphilia, characterized by a compulsive need to expose one's body, particularly the genital organs, as a means of achieving sexual excitement. The act is usually performed by a male in the presence of a female, children or unsuspecting adults. It is accompanied by masturbation. The surprise, fear and horror aroused in this act gives him the extra thrill he needs to achieve erection and ejaculation. In some instances exposure of the genitals is accompanied by suggestive gestures or masturbatory activity but more commonly there is only exposure.

Its main causes are:

1. *Personal Immaturity*

    Such exhibitionists seem to have inadequate information, feels shy and inferiority in approaching the opposite sex. They are immature in their sex role development, even though they may be well educated and competent in other life areas. Some have doubts and fears about their masculinity, combined with a strong need to demonstrate masculinity and potency.

2. *Inter-Personal Stress*

    Married exhibitionist appears to be reacting to some conflict or stress situation in his marriage.

3. *Association with other Psychopathology*

    Exhibitionist is associated with sociopathic personality disorder. Such individuals have a history of poor school adjustment and erratic work records. Often they have had difficulties with authorities as consequence of other antisocial acts. Their exhibitionism appears to be just one more form or antisocial behaviour to achieve sexual excitation and gratification. In some cases it is related with schizophrenic reactions.

Fetishism

It is also a psychosexual disorder in which sexual

gratification is repeatedly or exclusively achieved through fondling, kissing or licking inanimate objects such as woman's shoes or undergarments, garters or locks of hair. Handling these objects often accompanied by sexual fantasies and masturbation. In order to obtain the required object, the fetishist may commit burglary, theft or even assault. The articles most commonly stolen by fetishists are women's underthings.

Many stimuli can come to be associated with sexual excitation and gratification. Most people are stimulated to some degree by intimate articles of clothing and by perfumes and odours associated with the opposite sex. It causes conditioning experience. Fetishistic patterns of sexual gratification usually become the preferred patterns only when they are part of a larger picture of maladjustment.

Amputation fetishism, Anal fetishism, Breast fetishism, Foot fetishism and Shoe fetishism are also its parts.

❏❏

Common Questions for Adolescents

Q.1 Why do people have sex?

Ans. The term sex is derived from the Latin word *sexus,* which means to cut or to divide. Sex is the natural way of ensuring the continuation of species. Animals never think about it, they only respond to chaning levels of sex hormones which stimulate the reproductive urge. But as far as human beings are concerned it is made complicated by thoughts and feelings. We have sex because it gives us pleasure. Sex is the center of a loving relationship, a true bond between two people. The basic sex drive is a universal experience, but what turns people on differes from culture to culture. The rules and customs which govern sexual behaviour vary enormously from place to place.

Q.2 Why do people feel embarrassed while discussing sex?

Ans. Sex has been associated for so long with unacceptable and dirty feelings. Embarrassment also comes from the secrecy surrounding the sexual act. Our religious preachers always preach to abstain from sex and observe abstinence to attain salvation. A *brahamchari* is respected in the Hindu society. But in societies where sex has been open and free from ideas of guilt, it is accepted much more easily as being normal and natural.

Q.3 Why do boys enjoy looking at the pictures of naked women?

Ans. Generally boys and men can become sexually aroused when looking at pictures of naked women, blue films and by having sexual fantasies. Sexual arousal is a pleasurable feeling. So they enjoy looking at such type of materials.

Q.4 If any boy or girl is not very interested in sex, are they normal?

Ans. There is no fixed age when boys or girls suddenly become interested in sex. The way they feel has a lot to do with the level of sex hormones which are estrogens in girls and testotrones in boys. As the primary sex characteristics and organs produce more hormones, awareness of sexuality will gradually increase and then you will also become aware of the sexuality of others. Physical features directly involved in sexual behaviour and reproduction: the gonads (testes and ovaries) and the external sex organs (penis and vagina) are known as primary sex characteristics.

Q.5 Are the girls who carry contraceptives promiscuous?

Ans. Promiscuity is a casual and unselective sexual relation with a variety of partners, often without obtaining full sexual satisfaction. But this does not apply to the girl who carries contraceptives. Frankly speaking she is accepting responsibility for her actions. She cares both for herself and her boyfriends.

Q.6 If a girl feels sexy for more than one boy at a time,

does it mean she is nymphomaniac?

Ans. Nymphomania is a compulsive, insatiable need for sexual stimulatin and gratifucation in women, frequently leading to promiscuity or to masturbation performed several times a day. But in this case it simply means that she is young and healthy. Hormone activity around puberty makes a young person feel very sexually excited at times.

Q.7 If you want to have sex with someone, are you in love?

Ans. Love and sex are two different things. You do not have to be in love to be turned on by someone. People are often drawn to each other sexually, even though they know they could never really love each other. After puberty boys and girls begin to develop their own sexuality. They may find themselves attracted to other people, like their classmates, friends, teachers and even complete strangers. This intensity of feeling may be overwhelming. It takes time and experience to adjust to these new emotions.

Q.8 What type of sex is wrong?

Ans. It depends upon person's own attitude towards sex in general. There is no check-list. The only hard and fast rule is that sex must always be voluntary and never be violent No one should force something on the other.

Q.9 Why do people have sex with prostitutes?

Ans. The are many reasons why people go to prostitutes. They may be feeling lonely, or trapped in an unhappy marriage, They may not want emotional involvement in their sexual relationship or just for pleasure.

Q.10 What is sexual perversion?

Ans. Sexual perversion is that sexual behaviour which is culturally, morally and legally unacceptable. In simple words, it is the sexual behaviour which is extreme and anti-social, also these unusual sexual activities would shock or offend most people.

Q.11 What is sexual harassment?

Ans. It refers to repeated and unwanted sexual comments, looks, suggestion or physical contact which make one feel uncomfortable. It is very common throughout the world.

Q.12 Why do girls have periods?

Ans. A Periods or menstruation is the discharge of blood and tissue from the lining of the uterus, which has been built up in anticipation of implantation of a fertilized egg. It is a unique plan of nature for reproduction. Through this method the uterus is made ready each month for pregnancy. If conception does not take place and the egg is not fertilized, this lining breaks down and together with a small amount of blood, it is shed in the menstrual period.

The blood that comes out of vagina is not a sign that anything is wrong. A girl starts to menstruate when she begins puberty. This can be any time between the age of 9 and 18. The average age is about 13. The number of days between each period is governed by the production of hormones and this varies from person to person. Very few girls have completely regular periods. Although it is inconvenient to have irregular periods, but it is not abnormal.

During this period many girls and women feel discomfort, tension and irritability. It is a good idea to use a tampon or a sanitary towel for extra protection. This is a particular good time to exercise.

Q.13 What is clitoris and where is it?

Ans. clitoris is the most sensitive part of the female genitals. Girls may be less aware of their sexual organs than boys because their external organs are smaller and less obvious. Clitories is full of nerve endings. When stimulated it becomes stiff like an erect penis and pokes out of its hood. Stimulating the clitoris helps many women to have an orgasm.

Q.14 What is orgasm?

Ans. Orgasm is the peak or climax of sexual excitement and pleasure during which ejaculation of semen occurs in the male and vicinal contraction in the female. The peak period lasts less than one minute for most males and females. To have an orgasm you need to be sexually aroused. Your clitoris or penis needs to be rubbed and stimulated until the feeling of pleasure and sexual tension becomes very strong. At orgasm this tension is suddenly released. This can send waves of intense pleasure through your whole body. Men experience orgasm more often than women.

Q.15 Can any girl make her breasts grow bigger?

Ans. There is nothing one can do to hasten the growth of breasts. If anyone tries to sell you creams guaranteed to increase breast size then he is taking you for a ride. Exercise is also no help either since there are no muscles in the breast tissue itself. The size of the breasts makes no difference when you become pregnant. During pregnancy, the glands become larger to prepare for lactation.

Q.16 Do all men ejaculate?

Ans. All men do not ejaculate. There are physical and psychological reasons why some men are unable to ejaculate. In their case, the unused sperms just disintegrate and are absorbed harmlessly into the body. Ejaculation is not possible without erection. Erection usually provides the signals needed for ejaculation.

Q.17 Can I do something to stop erection when there are other people around?

Ans. Sometimes boys have erection at the most unexpected and awkward moments. Not only thought of a girl or sight of a girl but intense emotions like fear or anger and even strenuous physical exercise may give you an erection. In such a situation distract yourself by thinking of something that takes your mind off it. That is why there is a joke that penis have an annoying habit of becoming erect at the wrong time and refusing to erect at the right time.

Q.18 Do semen and pee ever get mixed?

Ans. Semen never comes out when you pee as there is a special valve value which automatically shut of urine when the penis is erect.

0.19 Why do boys and girls masturbate?

Ans. Masturbation helps relieve some of the sexual tension that is an inevitable part of growing up. Both boys and girls masturbate. Boys masturbate more than girls because the penis is more accessible and they are more used to touching it.

Masturbation is not bad for health in anyway. But always remember that masturbation should not become compulsive.

Girls and women masturbate mostly with their hands, rubbing against the sensitive ,clitoris at the top of the vulva. They may use a firm action over the whole vulva. Sometime using one or more fingers to enter the vagina and mimic the rhythmic movements of intercourse.

Q.20 What causes erection?

Ans. It is some kind of sexual signal which causes the penis to become erect. Sometimes it is caused by an erotic photograph or by the sight of a pretty girl; sometimes just the thought of a girl or of love making is enough to make it happen. But morning erection, commonly experienced by men upon awakening, is usually because of the pressure of a full bladder.

Q.21 Who is impotent?

Ans. A man who is unable to have an erection or to maintain it long enough to have sex is termed as impotent. It is a psychological problem which depends upon various factors. If a boy has had, a bad experience with a girl, he may not be able to have an erection the next time he tries to have sex.

Q.22 What is a condom?

Common Questions for Adolescents / 113

Ans. A condom is a thin rubber sheath which unrolls to fit over a man's erect penis. It can be used during sexual intercourse between a man and a woman. It helps prevent the woman from becoming pregnant and lowers the risk of sexually transmitted infection.

A condom must be put on before the penis touches vaginal area of the woman and it must be kept on until the penis is fully out of the vagina. A condom can only be used once. After it has been used, it should be wrapped in a tissue and throw in a dust bin. With a little practice, condoms are easy to use. They can be bought from a chemist shop and they are freely distributed at Family Planning Centres.

Condoms are safe, but they need to be used carefully. A tear in the condom could be disastrous. Make sure no air gets trapped when the condom is rolled over the erect penis.

Q.23 Why is it advised to consult a doctor before using a pill?

Ans. The contraceptive pill contains the female hormones estrogen and progesterone. They are designed to prevent ovulation by stopping the ova (eggs) from maturing in the ovaries. As it contains powerful hormones which interrupt the normal monthly cycle. Women should only take it under medical supervision. The doctor can keep a watch on its side effects.

Q.24 What is sterilisation?

Ans. It is a permanent method of contraception for both

men and women. Sterilisation makes the person sterile so they cannot start a baby.

Male sterilisation is called vasectomy. It involves closing off both of the vasdeferens so that sperm cannot travel into the man's urethra and out of his penis. After this operation, the person can still have erections, ejaculate and enjoy sex in the same way that he did before he was sterilised. The only difference is that now his semen contains no sperms. It is a very tiny operation taking only about 15 minutes. It is done under local anaesthesia, so there is no pain. Our Government is encouraging this method of family planning by offering a number of incentives.

Female sterilisation involves closing off both fallopian tubes so that ova cannot travel into the uterus. This means that the woman cannot get pregnant. But she still has menstural periods and she can enjoy sex in the same way that she did before she was sterilied.

But these are suitable only for those who are absolutely sure that they don't want any more children and that they won't change their mind later on.

Q.25 How would you know if you are pregnant or not?

Ans. To find out whether you are pregnant or not, go to a doctor or hospital or any family planning clinic. Pregnancy test cannot be done until 14 days after your last period was due. If the test is positive, you are pregnant. A negative result is not a clear signal. You will need to wait another four or five days and then have yourself tested again to be absolutely sure.

Q.26 What is AIDS?

AIDS stands for Acquired Immune Deficiency Syndrome. If you have AIDS, your body's immune system breaks down and it cannot fight off infections. AIDS is caused by a virus called HIV. You cannot catch AIDS but you can be infected with HIV. Experts think that most people with HIV eventually get HIV related symptoms or AIDS.

The two main ways in which this disease is passed on are:

- By direct sexual contact.
- By getting infected blood into your blood stream.

  You cannot catch the virus from toilet seats or from things like utensils or towels used by an AIDS victim. This deadly virus is known to be transmitted from the mother to the unborn child in the womb or at birth. or to a baby through the mother's milk.

Q.27 What is rape?

Ans. When any man forces another person (usually a woman) to have sexual intercourse against her will, it is known as rape. The man who rapes someone is called a rapist. Rape is a horrible crime. It is usually violent and very frightening for the person being raped. The victim is often known to the rapist.

Q.28 What is oral sex?

Ans. Oral sex is a general term for use of the lips, mouth, tongue and throat cavity in sexual stimulation and gratification. The various types of oral sex include kissing, sucking, biting, licking, exploring the partner's genital organs and erogenous zones with the tongue and swallow the partner's sexual secretions. when a woman has her genitals kissed, licked or sucked by someone, it is called cunnilingus. When a man has his penis kissed, licked or sucked by someone, it is called fellatio. There is a very small risk of catching HIV through oral sex. That is the reason why it has become so popular in these days.

Q.29 Are wet dreams harmful in any way?

Ans. Wet dreams are not harmful in any way. They are only a sign that your reproductive organs are developing and they can happen quite often during puberty. But don't worry if you don't have them because that is normal too.

Q.30 What is the thr-eoctrine Signature?

Ans. Throughout the world many people still believe that outward appearace of a substance represents its inner concept. Certain objects that outwardly resemble sexual organs are believed to have aphrodisiac effects. Examples are Rhinoceros Horn or Oyster that resemble penis and vagina respectively. Olives represent testes and cooked Okara represents vaginal lubrication.

An aphrodisiac is that substance that is alleged to stimulate sexual desire and activity. It is possible that suggestion plays a major part when they appear to have an effect.

Q.31 What are the effects of antisex indoctrination?

Ans. Antisex indoctrination is the instilling of negative attitude towards sex, especially in children. Many parents as a result of their own inhibitions, hangups or religious belief raise their children in a cool atmosphere in which cuddling, caressing and touching are discouraged or even punished. They keep their children in total ignorance of sexual matters and oppose sex education not only at home but in school too. These attitudes lay the ground work for sexual conflicts. frigidity and impotence in many instances.

Q.32 Why do some people feel inadequate while doing sex?

Ans. A person may be a millionaire, a world leader, an athlete, a wrestler or a distinguished scientist but may still feel inadequate doing a simple act of sex that is common for animals and birds.

It is because animals and birds never think about it. They just respond to changing levels the of sex hormones which stimulate or curb their reproductive urge. But in the case of men and women, instincts have been crippled by anxiety resulting from negative preconditioning normally based on expectations of family and society.

Q.33 What is sexual rejuvination?

Ans. Sexual rejuvination is the restoration of youthful sexual vigour among the ageing. An untold number of substances exercises and treatments have been tried but found wanting. Among them are downright frauds like radio-active water, X-ray lamps and various pills and potions.

Q.34 What is sex counselling?

Ans. Sex counselling is the guidance provided to an individual or couple by a sex therapist, social worker, psychiatrist, or doctor on questions such as conception, family planning, infertility, fear of failure in performance, unresponsiveness, sexual anatomy and physiology and techniques of intercourse.

Q.35 What is the sex centre of the brain?

Ans. Sex centre of the brain is a term sometimes applied to a small area at the base of the brain which is believed to control the sex drive and various sexual functions, including the ovulation cycle in the female and ejaculation in the male. Its principal component is the pituitary gland, the MASTER GLAND that programs not only the sex glands but every other gland in the body. Studies have also suggested that damage in this area may be one of the causes of nymphomania and satyriasis on the one hand and impotence and diminished sex interest on the other hand.

Satyriasis is a male sexual disorder characterised by an obsessive insatiable desire for sexual gratification. Nymphomania is a compulsive insatiable need for sexual stimulation and gratification in women, frequently leading to promiscuity or to masturbation performed several times a day.

❏❏

PARENTING

FAMILY & RELATIONS

  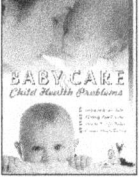   

COOKING

Also available in Hindi

HOUSEKEEPING

WOMEN ORIENTED

CLASSIC SERIES

Contact us at sales@vspublishers.com

GENERAL HEALTH & BEAUTY CARE

FITNESS

PERFECT HEALTH & AYURVEDA

A Set of 4 Books

DISEASES & COMMON AILMENTS

      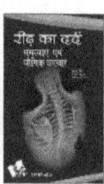

REGIONAL LANGUAGE

(Telugu)   (Odia)   (Marathi)   (Bangla)

MISCELLANEOUS

All books available at **www.vspublishers.com**

www.ingramcontent.com/pod-product-compliance
Lightning Source LLC
Chambersburg PA
CBHW070517100426
42743CB00010B/1845